THE DAILY
NUGGET

Praise for *The Daily Nugget*

"I believe all parents, coaches, and leaders should read and have a copy of *The Daily Nugget*! It gives an annual outline of coaching nuggets. I use it with my players and coaches daily. A MUST HAVE!!

—Ganon Baker
Global professional player development coach
Partner/Executive Director of Elev|8 Prep School

"*The Daily Nugget* is a treasure trove of inspiration for any coach, teacher, parent or player. Jim Burson is one of the finest teachers I have ever known, of the game and of life. Burson's lessons don't just motivate, they inspire in a sustained manner, and you'll understand exactly why you should act. He doesn't just tell you, he makes you deeply feel the lessons and they stay with you. *The Daily Nugget* is an amazing book by an amazing coach and man."

—Jay Bilas
ESPN

"The Daily Nugget gives coaches a positive approach to uplift players and themselves. A nugget a day will help you build your team in a powerful way."

—Jon Gordon
Best-selling author of *The Energy Bus*,
Training Camp and *The Carpenter*

The Daily Nugget, by best-selling author Jim Burson, fills the bill for essential coach and player preparation. In my opinion, coaches and players must develop background in two areas in order to maximize their chances for success:

1. Aspire to become a master teacher. It is not what we know and teach that is critical, but what students and players learn. John Wooden admonished all adults to set this as a pinnacle goal for success.

2. Inspire and motivate ourselves and others we lead and work with. Our best example serves as a fundamental tool for inspiring others to do the right thing.

Burson's book will help us in both areas. I recommend it highly for all who strive to reach their potential.

—Jerry Krause, EdD
NABC Research Chair

"Coach Burson continues to shed new light on fundamental areas of coaching that others have failed to explore. Nugget after nugget is filled with priceless wisdom and advice. We as readers become the rich benefactors of the Burson teachings."

—**George Raveling**
Director of International Basketball, Nike
Naismith Basketball Hall of Fame and John W. Bunn
Lifetime Achievement Award
National Collegiate Basketball Hall of Fame
CoachingForSuccess.com

"Every coach has an offensive and defensive system. Good coaches have a rebound and fast break system as well. But **great** coaches have a motivation and relationship system in place. *The Daily Nugget* is your motivation and relationship guide."

—**Jim Seward**
Owner of School of Hoops
National Association of Basketball Coaches board member *(retired)*
600+ college victories

"Coach Burson has served as both a friend and a mentor to me over the past 10+ years and has had a profound impact on my life as a coach. His new book, *The Daily Nugget*, shares so much of the wisdom and expertise I've learned from him – it is an absolute must read for any coach looking to master their craft and positively influence their players."

—**Alan Stein**
Owner of Stronger Team
Professional basketball performance coach

"Coach Burson has compiled an excellent package of affirmations, slogans, and coaching thoughts that can be invaluable in developing communication techniques of coaches and leaders in all walks of life. When the author's clearly presented programs are followed daily, you will acquire the tools to become a better leader, better communicator, and better coach. I urge you to rush to Amazon and get your copy now....it is never too early to begin preparations for next season and this book will help your preparation immensely."

—**Glenn Wilkes**
National Collegiate Basketball Hall of Fame
Owner of Basketball's Best and World-Class Basketball
Author of *The Complete Book on the Flex Offense*

THE DAILY NUGGET

Motivations for Basketball Coaches and Everyone Who Loves the Game

JIM BURSON

ABOUT THE AUTHOR

Dr. James Burson, creator of Solution-Based Basketball®, is known as a "coaches coach" for his lifetime commitment to the game. Jim is a consultant to basketball coaches and to sports companies, a popular motivational speaker, former president of the National Association of Basketball Coaches and a member of the Ohio Basketball Hall of Fame. He taught and coached for more than 40 years at the university level and is the author of *The Golden Whistle – Going Beyond: The Journey to Coaching Success.*

For George Raveling

A friend and mentor for the past 40 years. He has guided and lifted, enriched and encouraged me on my life's journey, as he has for so many coaches. George, you are a true giver. Thanks for your love, support and friendship. You have enriched me indeed.

For Jennifer Sue Lyle (Burson)

When I was hurt and struggling, she was sent to me. She is my wife, my best friend, my source of true joy and the CEO of our company. Without her, nothing makes sense. Thanks for lifting me up and for caring for me every day. 143.

*"When you study, really study!
When you play, play hard!"*

– Bob Tucker, my coach at Marysville High School

CONTENTS

PREFACE

I was inspired to write this book when Nike asked me to create the Coaches Learning Academy for their elite coaches. During those two-day annual workshops I was privileged to work with 40 talented coaches who were hungry to learn more about the game.

One day I received an excited phone call from one of those coaches, Book Richardson. He said, "Coach, I've just been hired as an assistant at Xavier University! During the interview, I found myself thinking of all the things you've taught us over the past two summers. I can't thank you enough for the information, but more importantly, thank you for your support and being my friend."

This is what it's about: challenging and lifting others to become the best that they can be. What a great game we coach.

I asked the Academy coaches to go beyond the X's and O's in order to make the X's and O's work for them. I shared my own long habit of discussing a word of the day with my players, my amazing experience of weekly phone calls with Coach Woody Hayes discussing the essays of Ralph Waldo Emerson, and how these non-basketball experiences were directly related to making me a better coach and making my teams the best that they could possibly be.

That's when I had the idea to compile the thoughts, statements and words I'd developed over the years into a daily calendar for coaches, and I began writing. With the advent of digital books, my idea has now become a reality with this book, *The Daily Nuggets: Motivations for Basketball Coaches and Everyone Who Loves the Game*.

It is my sincere hope that these nuggets will inspire, lift and encourage you, and that, in turn, you do the same for all the young men and women you coach and teach.

I inspire. You inspire. We inspire. I – U – WE.

Have a great journey as you engage a new nugget every day.

Notes:

- *Emanuel "Book" Richardson stayed at Xavier for two years and as of this writing, has been at the University of Arizona since then.*

- *The Nike Coaches Learning Academy was the brainchild of George Raveling, Nike's then-Global Director of Basketball. He asked me to lead it because he knew that I had created and led successful camps for coaches. He also knew that I have a special passion for working with and helping coaches, which is the focus of my business, Solution-Based Basketball®.*

INTRODUCTION

PRE-GAME TALK

One of my best players was having a bad day in practice. I was trying to be patient. "This is stupid," muttered the player as the team trotted past me to repeat the drill for the fourth time. My patience vanished. I swung my head toward him and shot back, "No, **you're** stupid." Without another word, the player walked off the court, off the team and withdrew from school.

Words have power. I didn't mean to hurt the kid. When I was growing up I'd heard the statement, "Sticks and stones may break my bones but words can never hurt me." Oh yes, they can.

What if I'd said, "Hey, I know you're having a tough time at home. Why don't you have a seat and chill out for awhile. We'll talk after practice." Or even "No, the drill isn't stupid. But you're acting stupid and I know you're a smart kid, so what's going on with you?"

Words have power.

This story should not have happened, but it did – and it continues to happen every day. Few coaches have escaped this experience, or one very like it, because coaches aren't always aware of the power of words.

You're never going to eliminate incidents and problems. We're all human. However, you can prevent many problems and minimize the damage when incidents occur. You certainly don't want to lose a player from something you said in a moment of anger!

This is why I wrote *The Daily Nugget*. It's more than a book – it's a motivational program that will help and guide you and your players every day.

I can't stress enough the importance of the relationship between the coach and the players as the foundation for a successful team.

Good relationships develop from good communication. When you use *The Daily Nugget* as a discussion guide with your players, you'll have a common denominator for your communication, one that is specifically designed to foster deep, ongoing conversations and forge the bonds that lead to better basketball and better lives.

I've prepared 365 daily nuggets for you, one for each day of the year. Begin on whatever day you've acquired the book and continue from there. Each daily nugget consists of three interrelated ideas:

The Practice is a concept or action for you to apply.

The Game gives insight and clarity to The Practice.

Word Thought provides a focus for the day and countless ways to engage others.

In the section, "How to Engage the Daily Nuggets," you'll learn how to get the most out of the nuggets for you, your players and your program. You might even want to make sure each member of your team has his or her own copy of the book.

Many people think of the basketball season as the five or six months from pre-conference games to the tournaments. As every coach knows, the truth is there's never an off-season in basketball; you simply move from one phase to the next. I introduce each of these phases with ideas for keeping motivation alive through the pre-season, early season, mid-season, post-season, and summer season.

Every coach needs to have a philosophy and every coach and player needs to be clear about their core values. I've dedicated special weeks throughout the year to some of my own core values: Work, Class and Character, Paradox and Adversity. I've dedicated other special weeks to some of the great thinkers about life and basketball who have deeply influenced my own philosophy: John Wooden, Ralph Waldo Emerson, Michael Jordan and Woody Hayes.

THE WARMUP

Great coaches don't let anything happen by chance alone. Add to the power of your coaching by developing the habit of reading the nugget each day. Reflect on **The Practice**. Contemplate **The Game**.

Understand the **Word Thought**. Embrace it and make it your own. Empower yourself with this process. This will enrich your day.

Think beyond where you are to where you want to be. We all have hopes and dreams in coaching and in life. Contemplate what it will take to reach your destination but, even more important, to savor the richness of the journey. *The Daily Nugget* will be your guide.

Lift yourself as a coach and as a teacher. Allow yourself to be lifted daily by the nuggets. Search for the wisdom and share with your players. When you do this, you'll lift all those around you.

WARNING!

Reading the nuggets each day may not be helpful if you don't read, reflect, contemplate, engage and share the meaning.

THE OPENING TIP: How to Engage the Daily Nuggets

Some of the nuggets are directed to coaches, some are directed to players, and some are directed to both coaches and players. In other words, they are designed to share, to discuss and for communicating. Use the nuggets daily to reach out to each other – coach to players, players to players, team leader to team members, parents to children. This will develop and enhance all your relationships, and they'll grow in both good times and tough times. You'll enlighten and enrich the lives of everyone around you.

Your most rewarding experience comes when you discover and refine your own ideas about each nugget. Use the following tips to help you engage them:

- Re-read the introduction to this book. Think about how you will engage the nuggets for yourself, your team and in your life.

- Read, ponder, study, expand and engage these ideas each day. Share them with anyone who wants to listen, but especially with your team.

- Use the day's nugget to begin each day or each practice in a positive and uplifting way. This will set the tone for your attitude and will influence those around you.

- Think about how the ideas apply to your team and to your individual situation. Develop your own practice and make it your own.

- Make it a habit to study the complete meaning of every Word Thought. You may want to look it up in the dictionary to find deeper meanings and uses. For example, the word "pressure" can begin a great conversation.

- I – U – WE: I get better – YOU get better – WE get better. At the end of the pre-practice talk, gather the players around you and have everyone, on the count of three, yell, "I – U – WE!" This is also great to use before games or at the end of time outs.

- Bring the day's nugget to your practice.

- If you're a head coach, lead pre-practice discussions about how each idea applies to your team. Give your assistants and players an opportunity to lead some of these discussions.

  » If you're a player, you can ask your coach to add nugget discussions to your pre-practice talks.

  » Define and talk about the Word Thought with players, other coaches, fans, friends and family.

  » Challenge the players to make the Word Thought apply to themselves and the team.

  » Write the daily Word Thought at the top of the practice schedule.

  » Be creative with your motivational approach.

- Create a Nugget Huddle: a group of coaches, players or friends to meet weekly to discuss the nuggets. You can do this in a Google chat, on Skype or even the old-fashioned way, in person.

- In my first book, *The Golden Whistle*, the first of the ten golden nuggets is titled "The Big Word Offense" and the word I used to describe it is "beyond." [1] This can lead to a great discussion with your team. What does it mean to go 'beyond' where your team is now and where they want to go?

Taking notes is the most important way you can engage the nuggets. If you want to get full value from this book, you'd better take notes! Use the note-taking section after each nugget – or do it the "old coach" way: Get a notebook, name it "Nugget Notebook," and write your notes there.

Research tells us that we retain more when we write than when we type, but either way – take the notes, and think about how this can help you, the players, and the team.

Have fun. Engage the nuggets. Enrich your life. Let this be the impetus you need to lift the lives of all those around you. Happy nugget-hunting in the wonderful world of words!

---

[1] *The Golden Whistle – Going Beyond: The Journey to Coaching Success;* Golden Nugget No. 1, 'The Big Word Offense: Our words reflect what is really in our heart.'

MID-SEASON

January – February – March

Happy New Year!

The beginning of the nuggets is in the middle of the basketball season. The excitement has settled and the grind begins. All teams have problems, concerns, excitement, and lots of games left to play.

This is the time that coaches and players need to really come together to form a bond, lead each other and develop toughness for the finish line. Christmas is over, and there are not many surprises left, but there is still a whole lot of working hard, knowing your roles and believing in each other.

I hear the distant sounds of the NCAA tournament and of high school tournaments on the road to the finals. Snap your fingers; it will be here soon!

Keep believing in yourself and your team. Keep reading, studying and engaging *The Daily Nugget.*

You are doing a great job, coach! Keep up the good work.

Find the gold in the grind!

JANUARY

Find the Gold in the Grind in January: What's the difference between a quote and a nugget? A quote is fleeting and doesn't resonate or stick in your mind or heart. You might just think, "That's nice," and go on. A nugget, however, enriches and deepens your view of life every day. It changes you. It changes how you operate, it changes how you think, it turns you into a better coach, it turns you into a better person. It will change your life – if you allow it to, if you accept it and do something with it.

Remember: to get full value, take notes each day. Use the note-taking section after each nugget or have your "Nugget Notebook" at your side.

January 1

The Practice
To navigate simply means to steer yourself toward your goal. You have to have clear goals and directions to accomplish all you can in basketball and in life.

The Game
Where do you want to go in the game? The higher your goals, the harder you must work. Be realistic and yet don't be afraid to dream. Don't lose sight of your life's goals. Always keep your academics first.

Word Thought
NAVIGATE

*Notes*_____

_____

_____

COACHING TIP FROM COACH BURSON:

Using January 1 as an example, here are some ideas for how to engage every nugget.

For yourself

As you read, ask yourself, "What are my goals for my personal life (family, friends, spirituality)? What are my goals for my basketball program? For my coaching development?

The goals you write down might look like these:

Personal – express my love to my family more frequently, set aside daily time for prayer or meditation.

Basketball – help my players develop leadership, achieve the top 3 of our conference.

Coaching development – strengthen my interpersonal skills, become an expert in special situations.

With your team

Does each player have a copy of the book? If so, encourage them keep a "Nugget Notebook." If not, could your booster program fund the purchase of a book (and notebooks) for every team and staff member?

Use the Word Thought NAVIGATE as the topic of your pre-practice conversation. Ask the players to take turns responding to and discussing these questions: What are my basketball goals? What are my academic goals? Who's navigating my ship in my basketball development? Who's navigating my academics ship? Who's in charge when things go wrong? If I don't feel that I'm navigating my own ship in basketball or academics or the rest of my life, who is? What can I do to make changes?

The great news – you get to do this every day with yourself and with your team!

January 2

The Practice

If you don't know where you are going, how will you know when you get there?

The Game

Setting realistic goals is one of the most important things you can do in basketball and in life. Its a new year. You may need to reset your goals. You must be clear on where you are today. You may need to define and refocus your goals. You must be clear!

Word Thought
GOAL

*Notes*_____

_____

_____

January 3

The Practice

Not worrying about winning helps prevent losing.

The Game

We spend a lot of time worrying about things that will not make us better. Do the best you can do with what you have. Toughness is more mental than physical. Have you read Jay Bilas' book, *Toughness*?

Word Thought
MENTAL TOUGHNESS

*Notes*_____

_____

_____

January 4

The Practice
It's often bad on the winner's side too.

The Game
The grass isn't always greener on the other side, but it is usually greener where you water it. Don't worry too much about the other players. Just keep practicing hard and smart.

Word Thought
PERSPECTIVE

*Notes*_____

_____

_____

January 5

The Practice
Control your thoughts and emotions or they will control you.

The Game
You must discipline yourself not to react to others. Be strong in your mind and your body will be strong.

Word Thought
REACTIONS

*Notes*_____

_____

_____

ADVERSITY WEEK
January 6 – 12

The best coaches face adversity. It will be a constant companion of anyone who enters the coaching profession. "Situations and circumstances be damned!" You must be strong in the face of your concerns and practices. Have a great week engaging your adversity.

– *The Golden Whistle*, Golden Nugget No. 7

The Practice

Accept whatever comes. The only important thing is that you meet it with courage and the best you have to give. This is how you work through adversity.

The Game

Some things you can't change, but you can always control how you react to the change.

Word Thought

ADVERSITY

*Notes*_____

_____

_____

Adversity Week

The Practice
You can take a setback and turn it into a comeback.

The Game
Whether you win or lose, you must be able to control your reactions.

Word Thought
SETBACK

*Notes*_____

_____

_____

Adversity Week

The Practice
You can't get anywhere today if you are bogged down in yesterday.

The Game
Be realistic, evaluate what happened yesterday, then make adjustments. Let go and move on to another bridge in life.

Word Thought
BOGGED

*Notes*_____

_____

_____

Adversity Week   January 9

The Practice

A diamond is a piece of coal that handled the pressure and became more valuable.

The Game

How you handle tough pressure situations will determine whether you become more valuable to your team and in life.

Word Thought

VALUABLE

*Notes*_____

_____

_____

Adversity Week   January 10

The Practice

It may not be your fault for being down, but it's your fault for not getting up.

The Game

The great players get knocked down just like everyone does, but they just always get back up and become stronger.

Word Thought

FAULT

*Notes*_____

_____

_____

Adversity Week   January 11

The Practice

A gem cannot be polished without friction, nor a player perfected without trials.

– Chinese proverb (paraphrase)

The Game

You are going to have people and situations rub you the wrong way. Let it make you shine even more!

Word Thought

FRICTION

*Notes*_____

_____

_____

Adversity Week   January 12

The Practice

When players worry about practice time and playing time and are constantly filled with doubts, no amount of coaching can help.

The Game

You must practice hard and let things fall as they will. It's hard not to worry and doubt a little, but you must be mentally strong to prepare and then practice hard.

Word Thought

WORRY

*Notes*_____

_____

_____

January 13

The Practice

Winning is not a place to get to but a state of mind.

The Game

Preparation is the key to being able to concentrate. You must believe you are good enough to win and that comes from working hard in practice.

Word Thought

CONCENTRATE

*Notes*_____

_____

_____

January 14

The Practice

Control your thoughts and emotions or they will control you.

The Game

It is easy to react in negative ways. As a competitor, it is often difficult to control your emotions. However, you can improve how you respond, but you must concentrate and want to do it.

Word Thought

RESPOND

*Notes*_____

_____

_____

January 15

The Practice

When you watch a game, be a student of the game.

The Game

Whether it is in person or on TV, evaluate and analyze what is going on. Gather knowledge whenever possible. You may be surprised where you find it.

Word Thought

KNOWLEDGE

*Notes*_____

_____

_____

January 16

The Practice

Great teams consist of players who work hard, work together and don't care who gets the credit.

The Game

It is easy to give lip service to putting the team's needs above your own. It's much more difficult to implant into one's heart. However, the difference in the way each of these attitudes impacts a team is as plain as night and day. Better yet, between winning and losing.

Word Thought

IMPLANT

*Notes*_____

_____

_____

January 17

The Practice
Adjust to changing times but cling to unchanging principles.

The Game
Being a player's coach is neat, but make sure you do the things that maintain your personal philosophy and integrity.

Word Thought
INTEGRITY

*Notes*_____

_____

_____

January 18

The Practice
If you make a turnover without knowing why you made it, you will probably make it again.

The Game
You will make turnovers in the game of basketball and in life. Being aware that you made a mistake will help you understand why you made it and allow you to work on not making it again.

Word Thought
AWARENESS

*Notes*_____

_____

_____

January 19

The Practice

If your philosophy doesn't win games, I don't want to hear about it.

The Game

Be careful here! What level do you coach? Do you want to win at all costs? Are there other factors involved? We all want to win, but keep everything in proper perspective.

Word Thought

PERSPECTIVE

*Notes*_____

_____

_____

January 20

The Practice

There is no better way to improve than with a well-organized practice and proper repetition of fundamentals.

The Game

You must organize practice, have proper drills in the right order and add variety, but be repetitive. You must help develop mental toughness.

Word Thought

ORGANIZE

*Notes*_____

_____

_____

January 21

The Practice
For a great coach or player, one turnover, one mistake can be critical.

The Game
Your ability to demand excellence may be your edge. One missed basket, one poor pass, one defensive let-up can make the difference in a game or a season.

Word Thought
EDGE

*Notes*_____

_____

_____

January 22

The Practice
Do not complain about circumstances. Take what you have and make the best of it.

The Game
Everyone is dealt a hand. How you play it is really important. Being positive in difficult situations can lift you and everyone around you.

Word Thought
CIRCUMSTANCES

*Notes*_____

_____

_____

January 23

The Practice

Hope and fear cannot alter the outcome of a season. However, hard work, great desire and well-organized practices – that's different!

The Game

Everyone gets down and feels afraid. It is at this time you are really vulnerable. You must be tough mentally and physically to eliminate fear and establish a solid program.

Word Thought

VULNERABILITY

*Notes*_____

_____

_____

January 24

The Practice

You must be a complete player on offense and defense. Be fundamentally sound and mentally strong so that you can take your game to new levels.

The Game

You must want to work on all phases of your game. Perhaps the mental phase will be the most difficult, but it's essential that you work on it to become a better player.

Word Thought

COMPLETE

*Notes*_____

_____

_____

January 25

The Practice
Nothing can help a player who has not overcome his doubts: not greater size, stronger body, playing more, lifting weights, or even studying the game day and night.

The Game
The great coach Bobby Knight said that the mental is to the physical as 4 is to 1. You must be four times tougher mentally than physically in order to overcome the doubts that everyone has at one time or another.

Word Thought
DOUBTS

*Notes*_____

_____

_____

January 26

The Practice
You must watch coaches carefully – how they live, eat, sit, talk and behave, both during the game and after. The component parts of all these make a coach what he truly is!

The Game
Coaching is an extension of your life. Be sure to be yourself. Study other coaches, take a little from each, but be yourself.

Word Thought
YOURSELF

*Notes*_____

_____

_____

January 27

The Practice

Keep your mind open and all the basketballs will pass through the net. Close your mind and all you will see are the misses.

The Game

You must always be willing to listen to others, always be willing to learn more in basketball and life. Never close your mind to new possibilities.

Word Thought

POSSIBILITIES

*Notes*_____

_____

_____

January 28

The Practice

You must allow, expect and accept some mistakes to happen in the game.

The Game

Understanding that mistakes will happen, making players aware of the mistake, and then giving them direction to lessen the chance of repeating the mistake is called the art of coaching.

Word Thought

UNDERSTANDING

*Notes*_____

_____

_____

January 29

The Practice
We think in wins and losses but live in fundamentals.

The Game
Let other people judge you by your record. Judge yourself by how much your team has improved fundamentally.

Word Thought
FUNDAMENTAL

*Notes*_____

_____

_____

January 30

The Practice
A great player thinks little! The player who over-thinks, reacts or becomes angry will defeat himself in games as well as life.

The Game
You cannot worry too much or get bogged down with reactions. Play your game and try not to be influenced by circumstances.

Word Thought
INFLUENCE

*Notes*_____

_____

_____

January 31

The Practice

It is better to see your game than to hear your game.

The Game

Don't tell me how good you are. Show me! Be able to back up whatever you say by practicing hard every day.

Word Thought

SHOW

Notes_____

_____

_____

Re-read the introduction to the Mid-Season.

FEBRUARY

Find the Gold in the Grind in February: Help others after a loss? We lost a tough away game and left for home, two hours away, at 10:30 pm, driving two station wagons in the worst snowstorm of the year. The mood was sullen and somber until one of the cars spun off the road into a ditch. Our players got out, pushed us back on the road and then, without being told, pushed about ten other cars out of the ditch and back on the road. We continued back to campus in a much better mood. Oh yes, the loss was still there, but helping, giving and sharing made it seem a whole lot less important. The experience had increased our energy and empowered our spirit. Engage in helping others and you will help yourself. Giving gets!

Remember: to get full value, take notes each day. Use the note-taking section after each nugget or have your "Nugget Notebook" at your side.

February 1

The Practice
Stay composed by accepting whatever you are doing. This is the ultimate achievement.

The Game
In the middle of bad calls, bad breaks and losses, it is difficult to stay focused, to stay positive. But if you can, you are a winner.

Word Thought
ACCEPTING

*Notes*_____

_____

_____

February 2

The Practice

Great defense requires less physical effort than you think and more mental toughness than you can imagine.

The Game

You must be strong mentally through hard work and hard practice. Toughness doesn't just happen. You must work at it.

Word Thought

IMAGINE

*Notes*_____

_____

_____

COACHING TIP FROM COACH BURSON:

How are you doing with your Word Thought discussions? This illustration might help. Ask yourself, your players and team to answer these questions:

- *Can you <u>imagine</u> how we might be able to get better?*
- *Can you <u>imagine</u> having a great practice today?*
- *Can you <u>imagine</u> a game with no "bad" calls by the officials?*
- *Can you <u>imagine</u> how much tougher we can become?*

I love to work my imagination into reality. Let's take one step today to get better. <u>Imagine</u> how good we might become.

I'm truly interested in hearing from you about your discussions. Drop me a note using the contact form at www.jimburson.com/contact.

February 3

The Practice

A great coach demands that players sprint, not jog, to both ends of the floor. Winning depends on which you do. Sprint, you win; jog, you lose.

The Game

It takes great conditioning and great dedication to sprint for 40 minutes. Be a 40-minute sprinter.

Word Thought

SPRINT

*Notes*_____

_____

_____

February 4

The Practice

Make a fine line of difference in your practices. That's what sets winning and losing apart.

The Game

You must take time to develop each practice. The difference seems insignificant, but it could be monumental.

Word Thought

INSIGNIFICANT

*Notes*_____

_____

_____

February 5

The Practice

When a great defensive player guards a great offensive player, all he sees is a way to steal the ball.

The Game

The challenge must always be to stop the offensive player, but ultimately steal the ball. Work hard on the defensive end.

Word Thought

CHALLENGE

*Notes*_____

_____

_____

February 6

The Practice

Fear of losing is often developed from the absence of faith that you can win.

The Game

The best way to eliminate your fears is through proper preparation. You want to develop your faith in yourself and your team, then practice like every day is a big game.

Word Thought

DEVELOP

*Notes*_____

_____

_____

February 7

The Practice

Don't tug on SuperMom's cape!

The Game

Moms will always love their kids more than you. Prepare to face the Tug Test.

Word Thought

LOVE

*Notes*_____

_____

_____

February 8

The Practice

The leading scorer who is proud of his points is like the condemned man who is proud of his cell.

The Game

Pride is a good thing but be careful – be sure and develop your whole game. Then you can be really proud.

Word Thought

PRIDE

*Notes*_____

_____

_____

February 9

The Practice

Toughness is found in doing what is right and not in getting what you want.

The Game

Nobody always gets what they want. True toughness comes from always doing what is right and best for yourself and the team.

Word Thought

TOUGHNESS

*Notes*_____

_____

_____

February 10

The Practice

Never let go of the reins of the wild colt in your heart.
– Buddhist proverb

The Game

You should always be young at heart, excited and fired up. However, don't go wild. Always keep a little control by holding tight to your reins and letting go only when needed!

Word Thought

CONTROL

*Notes*_____

_____

_____

February 11

The Practice

We will strive to have a perfect practice through having imperfect practice.

The Game

Most people will say you can never have a perfect practice, but we should never give up striving toward being as good as we possibly can be.

Word Thought

PERFECT

Notes

RALPH WALDO EMERSON WEEK
February 12 – 18

Woody Hayes stopped me in the hallway at St. John's Arena to congratulate me on getting my master's degree. I told him that I'd actually just finished my PhD.

He stuck his index finger in my chest and said in classic Woody Hayes style, "That will ruin your coaching! People will ask more out of you as a teacher and administrator! Read Ralph Waldo Emerson's *Essay on Compensation* and call me Monday at 10:00 AM. Let me know what the farmer and the president have in common!"

That was my introduction to Emerson and my many discussion with Coach Hayes about Emerson's essays! Emerson would have been a great basketball coach.

Engage the essays!

Ralph Waldo Emerson Week　　　February 12

The Practice
"We must be our own before we can be others."
– Ralph Waldo Emerson, "Friendship" *Essays: First Series* (1841)

The Game
You must know yourself and know that you will be compensated for exactly what you deserve; no more, no less.

Word Thought
COMPENSATION

*Notes*_____

_____

_____

Ralph Waldo Emerson Week — February 13

The Practice

There can never be true conversation, no true relationship, between a player and a coach, until each talks in terms of the team.

– Ralph Waldo Emerson, "Friendship" (paraphrase)

The Game

We get so wrapped up in winning, in our own ego, we forget it is really about working for the team to get better. I get better for **YOU**. **YOU** get better for me. **WE** get better for the team. **I U WE.**

Word Thought

CONVERSATION

*Notes*_____

_____

_____

Ralph Waldo Emerson Week — February 14

The Practice

You must love and respect other coaches, but be careful not to study their ideas so much that you lose your own.

– Ralph Waldo Emerson, "Friendship" (paraphrase)

The Game

Study other coaches, steal ideas, beg for help, copy great thoughts, then make them your own. Always make them your own.

Word Thought

IDEAS

*Notes*_____

_____

_____

The Practice

Winning has its tax, and if it comes without work and sweat, it has little virtue; the next game will blow it away!

– Ralph Waldo Emerson, "Compensation" (paraphrase)

The Game

You may not follow all the rules and still win, but the truth is known and the price must be paid in full. There are no shortcuts to success.

Word Thought

SHORTCUTS

*Notes*_____

_____

_____

The Practice

Winning reduces blame as surely as the sun melts the iceberg in the sea.

– Ralph Waldo Emerson, "Compensation" (paraphrase)

The Game

Winning only covers the problems unless you are doing things the right way. The blame will return. Blame **I**. Blame **YOU**. Blame **WE**. **I U WE**

Word Thought

BLAME

*Notes*_____

_____

_____

Ralph Waldo Emerson Week — February 17

The Practice

The question of how to coach resolves itself into a practical question of my conduct!! How should I live?

– Ralph Waldo Emerson, "Fate" (paraphrase)

The Game

Do as I say. Do as I do. Be the example on and off the floor. That sets a great example for how to live.

Word Thought

EXAMPLE

*Notes*_____

_____

_____

Ralph Waldo Emerson Week — February 18

The Practice

The fate of the team may be determined by a coach who thanks his bench and stands in some terror of his starters.

– Ralph Waldo Emerson, "Fate" (paraphrase)

The Game

A good coach appreciates all members of the team. He must prepare his bench to play and put his starters on the bench if needed.

Word Thought

APPRECIATE

*Notes*_____

_____

_____

February 19

The Practice

By your mistakes (turnovers) the game is perfected.

The Game

Every team and every person makes mistakes. However, you must never stop learning from your mistakes and trying to become the best you can be.

Word Thought

PERFECTION

*Notes*_____

_____

_____

February 20

The Practice

Coaching does not need to get rid of ego, but to transcend it.

The Game

There is a difference between cocky and confident. Being able to transcend ego to benefit the team is a coaching gem.

Word Thought

TRANSCEND

*Notes*_____

_____

_____

February 21

The Practice

"Our theories about who will win or lose are often as valuable as are those of a chick, which has not broken its way through its shell, might form of the outside world."
–Attributed to Buddha

The Game

Trying to figure out if you will win or lose is not as important as preparing for the game by practicing properly.

Word Thought

THEORY

*Notes*_____

_____

_____

February 22

The Practice

When the player is ready the coach will appear. The reverse is also true.

The Game

The coach and player must be on the same page. If they can work together, then it will be a lot easier for both to reach their full potential.

Word Thought

TOGETHERNESS

*Notes*_____

_____

_____

February 23

The Practice

The shots you miss provide more opportunities for the shots you will make.

The Game

Your attitude will carry you on those days when the shots just won't drop. Life is a lot like that too. Keep a positive attitude, keep working and good things will happen.

Word Thought

ATTITUDE

*Notes*_____

_____

_____

February 24

The Practice

If you are open to suggestions (coaching), you will always be ready to improve. In young players' minds, there are many possibilities. In older players, there are a lot less.

The Game

You must be willing to listen to new ideas, positive criticism and reinforcement. Sometimes it is difficult to hear that you have not measured up, but take it to heart and try again.

Word Thought

IMPROVEMENT

*Notes*_____

_____

_____

February 25

The Practice
The coach and player should equal unity and cooperation.

The Game
It is easy for the coach to dominate the situation, particularly with younger players. It is good to lead, but to carry the players along makes everything more enjoyable.

Word Thought
UNITY

*Notes*_____

_____

_____

February 26

The Practice
If you are too elated about winning, later you will be deflated about losing.

The Game
It is so easy to get wrapped up in winning, but we cannot get carried away. The same with losing. Keep these two components in proper perspective.

Word Thought
PERSPECTIVE

*Notes*_____

_____

_____

February 27

The Practice

A player who is physically powerful but lacks skills may be frustrating. But a coach who is well-spoken but does not practice what he preaches can damage lives.

The Game

You must be a person of your word. It is easy to talk the talk, but whether you are a coach or a player, you must also walk the walk.

Word Thought

PREACH

*Notes*_____

_____

_____

February 28

The Practice

Basketball is a game such that if you wish to enjoy its pleasures, you must also endure its pain.

The Game

As young is to old, as hot is to cold, as up is to down, so in practice you must work hard so that you can enjoy the game.

Word Thought

ENJOY

*Notes*_____

_____

_____

Re-read the introduction to the Mid-Season.

MARCH

Find the Gold in the Grind in March: Players want to be led. They want to know the coach can help give them direction. They want to believe in the coach and trust that he, too, is learning every day to help them become the best they can be. Even after a grinding practice or after a tough loss they must have hope that the coach can lead them on those little steps to improvement. The Daily Nugget *can lead you in the right direction.*

Remember: to get full value, take notes each day. Use the note-taking section after each nugget or have your "Nugget Notebook" at your side.

March 1

The Practice
Seeking perfection is like looking for footprints of birds in the sky.

The Game
You should strive to be the best you can. Reach high, work hard, but don't let failure or lack of perfection keep you from trying.

Word Thought
PERFECTION

*Notes*_____

_____

_____

March 2

The Practice

Some players are noisy on the outside and quiet on the inside.

The Game

A good coach knows both the physical and mental makeup of each player. Do not be fooled by appearances. Know the inner makeup of all your players.

Word Thought

APPEARANCES

*Notes*_____

_____

_____

March 3

The Practice

Perfect awareness of an imperfect shot is better than imperfect awareness of a perfect shot.

The Game

The only way to learn is from our imperfections. By being aware and paying attention at all times we can learn from all experiences – even our worst mistakes.

Word Thought

IMPERFECTION

*Notes*_____

_____

_____

March 4

The Practice
Are great shooters made or born?

The Game
Motor skills are not developed strictly from someone's genetic makeup. Developing those skills requires training at many levels: physical, mental, sensory, etc. To advance in any skill, one must commit time to develop, have the passion to persist, and amass the knowledge to evaluate and progress. Good shooters can be made, but you must understand that it's much more than just going out and shooting a lot.

Word Thought
COMMIT

Notes _____

_____

_____

March 5

The Practice
Confidence is hard to teach. It comes from one thing only: demonstrated ability.

The Game
You cannot wish confidence. You cannot dream it. You must accomplish it. Good shooters have short memories regarding their last miss. Their confidence doesn't waver. Confidence of success may be more important than any technique taught. Developing player confidence is an important part of coaching.

Word Thought
CONFIDENCE

Notes _____

_____

_____

March 6

The Practice

Great shooters never think about missing. Once the negative enters the mind, the chances for success are greatly diminished.

The Game

You cannot think about the consequences of missing a shot. Once you begin to think in terms of consequences, you think of a negative result.

Word Thought
CONSEQUENCES

*Notes*_____

_____

_____

March 7

The Practice

Remember this word when thinking about shot selection: RIPS

The Game

R = Range: Are you in yours?

I = In rhythm. On balance.

P = Pressure. Is the defense crowding you or is it a clean look?

S = Score and clock considerations.

Word Thought
SELECTION

*Notes*_____

_____

_____

March 8

The Practice
Any successful team is a reflection or a shadow of the leader!

The Game
The coach must lead, but a player needs to surface if the team is to reach its full potential.

Word Thought
POTENTIAL

*Notes*_____

_____

_____

March 9

The Practice
Success is setting a goal and accomplishing it. Significance is understanding how the goal was accomplished. We want significant players.

The Game
There are many players with tremendous athletic qualities and basketball skills. What separates the 'greats' and the 'super-greats?' Knowledge is one key. To not just execute a skill or play but to know the how's and why's takes players to a different level. Obtaining understanding is the separating factor. Teach your players understanding. Develop significant players.

Word Thought
SIGNIFICANCE

*Notes*_____

_____

_____

March 10

The Practice

Basketball is a game that gives you every chance to be great and puts every pressure on you to prove you don't have what it takes. This is true for coaches as well as players.

The Game

Life is a self-fulfilling prophecy. Nowhere is this more evident than on the court. You are always in a position to demonstrate ability and there is always the chance of failure. the game never takes away your opportunity to get better, but it never eases the pressure of potential failure.

Word Thought

PRESSURE

*Notes*_____

_____

_____

March 11

The Practice

Great players are the ones who hear what they don't want to hear, see what they don't want to see, and do what they don't want to do.

The Game

Taking coaching and correction in proper context is a skill in itself. Unfortunately, our culture encourages a lack of accountability in the individual. Being an accountable coach is the best way to develop accountability in your players.

Word Thought

ACCOUNTABILITY

*Notes*_____

_____

_____

March 12

The Practice

"The man of genius is he and he alone who finds such joy in his art that he will work at it come hell or high water."
– Stendhal (Marie-Henri Beyle)

The Game

Deep down there is something inside us that draws us to the game and what is required of it. There is joy in the grind. There is peace in the routine. There is pride in knowing that if it was easy, everyone would do it.

Word Thought
ROUTINE

*Notes*_____

_____

_____

March 13

The Practice

It is always safe to assume that there may be a better way, even when the old way is still working

The Game

Many times we coaches will ask players to change techniques that may have been very successful for them in the past. This is not out of disrespect to a previous coach; instead, it's simply to provide methods that may be a better fit for a different system.

Word Thought
DIFFERENT

*Notes*_____

_____

_____

March 14

The Practice

"Do not trust to the cheering, for those very persons would shout as much if you and I were going to be hanged."
– Oliver Cromwell

The Game

You must be careful of those who come forward as a friend only when you win or are successful. Fans are fickle and fame is fleeting. Choose friends wisely. Seek loyalty. Don't you just love the Game?

Word Thought

FICKLE

*Notes*_____

_____

_____

March 15

The Practice

Next in importance to having good aim is having the ability to recognize when to shoot the ball.

The Game

The greatest shooter in the world still cannot be effective without a basic understanding of good shot selection. This awareness and understanding builds confidence and prevents the 'what if' worries: 'what if I miss?'

Word Thought

SELECTION

*Notes*_____

_____

_____

March 16

The Practice

Practice like you are preparing for a game. You play the game to learn what to work on in the next practice so you will be ready for the next game!

The Game

Focus and concentrate during every practice. Work on fundamentals and repeat them until they become habits so you can utilize them in the pressure of the game. Strive for perfection in practice, seek perfection in the game. We know there can be no perfection, but keep trying every day. Coaching is such a great merry-go-round. Handle the ups and downs and keep going around.

Word Thought
MERRY-GO-ROUND

*Notes*_____

_____

_____

March 17

The Practice

Coaching and playing are a grindstone. Whether it grinds you down or polishes you up depends on what you are made of.

The Game

The schedule and demands of basketball are grindstones. For players, it is almost like obtaining a second college degree. How you handle the grind of being a student-athlete is a good indicator of how you'll deal with the hurdles of life.

Word Thought
GRIND

*Notes*_____

_____

_____

March 18

The Practice

The one permanent emotion of the inferior coach is fear – fear of the unknown, the complex, the inexplicable, of change. What they want more than anything is safety.

The Game

Fear is natural. How can you learn to manage it? How can you reduce fear's negative impact?

1. Collect sound information.
2. Give of your time.
3. Force an effort.
4. Respond to your analysis.

Apply these four steps to any skill or problem and it will lead to demonstrated ability and in turn develop true confidence.

Word Thought

FEAR

*Notes*_____

_____

_____

March 19

The Practice

I can give you three surefire ways to avoid being criticized: Do nothing. Say nothing. Be nothing.
– Elbert Hubbard (paraphrase)

The Game

Athletes are under the spotlight. The great ones love the arena, the competition and most importantly the risk.

Word Thought

CRITICISM

*Notes*_____

_____

_____

March 20

The Practice

"Nothing in the world can take the place of persistence. Talent will not; nothing is more common than unsuccessful men with talent .... Persistence and determination alone are omnipotent."
– Calvin Coolidge

The Game

There will be many times over your career when you will question whether all you go through is really worth it. Can you handle the regret of not knowing if just a little more time or effort would have changed your path? Own your next practice!

Word Thought

PERSISTENCE

*Notes*_____

_____

_____

March 21

The Practice

To the gifted young player: You have a tremendous talent that others don't have, but it's not enough. If you rely solely on your gift and don't develop it, you'll eventually fail.

The Game

Players with athleticism and skills are everywhere. Those who continue to learn and grow as players, and aren't satisfied with where they are now, truly separate themselves into a different level.

Word Thought

TALENT

*Notes*_____

_____

_____

March 22

The Practice

Shooting the basketball is like shaving. If you let it go for awhile, you're going to end up looking bad.

The Game

Fine motor skills, especially ones with as small a margin of error as shooting, require a commitment to maintain and develop them. Don't let shooting skills stagnate or regress through lack of practice. The first step of playing at the highest level is to be able to shoot the ball at the highest level.

Word Thought

REGRESS

*Notes*_____

_____

_____

March 23

The Practice

Defense doesn't always break down on the help. Often it breaks down on the recovery.

The Game

Technique vs. athleticism on defense is important. If you are superior in size, strength and quickness to your opponent, then technique is often moot. But what if your opponent is the superior athlete? What if your opponent is equal in these areas? Proper technique such as close-outs separate the equal teams and surprise the superior teams.

Word Thought

TECHNIQUE

*Notes*_____

_____

_____

March 24

The Practice
Great efforts spring naturally from great attitudes.

The Game
Who ultimately controls your attitude? What are the factors that eat away at a good attitude? How do you deal with the inevitable ups and downs of coaching? Of being an athlete? If you have a hard time answering these questions, you're going to have a hard time finding the effort required to succeed.

Word Thought
ATTITUDE

*Notes*_____

_____

_____

March 25

The Practice
Players don't care what you know about practice until they know how much you care about them.

The Game
Players, if you want to be a leader in your program, you must have the ability to convince your teammates you want them to succeed for the benefit of the team. Can you sincerely put the group's goals ahead of your individual ones? Can you really care about the needs of others before your own?

Word Thought
SINCERE

*Notes*_____

_____

_____

March 26

The Practice

Players who are late are telling their teammates and the coach that their time is more important than the team.

The Game

It may seem like a simple thing. It may seem to have little or no impact on winning. But the ability and the desire to be on time sends a winning message: I'm thinking for the team first and not my own needs.

Word Thought

MESSAGES

*Notes*_____

_____

_____

March 27

The Practice

What do you do with a mistake?
1. Recognize it
2. Admit it
3. Learn from it
4. Forget it

The Game

None of these four is easy to do. Self-analysis is tough. Admitting mistakes publicly is really tough. Breaking old habits so as not to repeat mistakes is really, really tough. Letting mistakes go so as to focus on the next play is really, really, really tough. But you can do it!

Word Thought

MISTAKES

*Notes*_____

_____

_____

March 28

The Practice

There are two things while playing basketball you can't do too much of. You can pass, shoot or dribble too much, but I've never been able to think of a situation where you rebound too much or communicate too much.

1. Rebound endlessly.
2. Communicate endlessly.

The Game

Talking to teammates properly and rebounding are not exactly skills that will get you headlines, but just try to win without these qualities. It's rare indeed to find that player who keeps people up, together and focused on the floor. Almost as rare is that player who is relentless on the boards.

Word Thought

RELENTLESS

*Notes*_____

_____

_____

March 29

The Practice

Basketball is all about sharing.

The Game

This is a short but powerful statement. The interconnection among teammates on a basketball team is unlike any other sport. Sharing the ball, helping a teammate get open, sharing your praise for those who help you make a play and, in turn, helping someone else make a play, helping on defense, accepting a role and helping a teammate accept theirs. These are just a few examples of how good teams blend together and succeed.

Word Thought

SHARE

*Notes*_____

_____

_____

March 30

The Practice

Good shooters take shots. The best shooters take most of the shots.

The Game

If you want a bigger role offensively, you must show people, not tell them. Establish that you are one of the best shooters (1) nightly in practice and (2) consistently in games. You must earn the right to be a shooter. It is not handed over on reputation or potential.

Word Thought

CONSISTENCY

*Notes*_____

_____

_____

March 31

The Practice

If you want your team to perform, you must stress defense. Defense makes players unselfish.

The Game

Defense is not so much about technique as it is about a mindset. Learning to play defense is not as fun as perfecting an offensive move. However, once a player attains the attitude of being a great defender, he fully understands the value of things that don't always catch the public eye. A great defender puts the team's welfare above his own ego.

Word Thought

DEFENSE

*Notes*_____

_____

_____

Re-read the introduction to the Mid-Season.

Mid-Season Summary

Review your notes from the Mid-Season and reflect on the events and insights that have taken place. Write down your answers to the following three questions on the lines below or in your "Nugget Notebook."

What did you learn from the Mid-Season Daily Nuggets?

_____

_____

_____

Are you ready for the Post-Season?

_____

_____

_____

Which Word Thought was most important for you and why? Keep using that word going forward.

_____

_____

_____

POST-SEASON

April – May

---

*"Spectacular achievement is always
preceded by unspectacular preparation."*

– Robert Schuller

Give some time off so everyone can recover from the battles of the season. How much time off? A week? Two weeks? What activities are permitted under the rules that govern your program?

Under any rules, you could send or post *The Daily Nugget* so that you and your players can stay in touch. Other helpful activities include:

- Conduct individual meetings with players

- Evaluate individuals, including assistant coaches and team managers

- Prepare an assessment of the team's strengths and weaknesses

- Review game tapes

- Start to feel the "NEXT" season coming

Coach, you must make sure the players keep their heads screwed on right both socially and academically. Use **The Practice** and **The Game** and **Word Thought** – bend them to fit the time and situations that are most helpful to each player.

There really is no off-season! There is only a change in season and you must stay on top of all situations and circumstances that involve the players. One of the best ways to be proactive and stay on top is through daily communication.

This is a great time for the players to exhibit and focus on self-motivation – intrinsic motivation to do the little extra things that great players and teams do that separate them from the average players and teams. You can help them with this by using *The Daily Nugget*.

Lift the weights. Work on the skills. Emphasize the academics. Don't you just love coaching?!

P.S. Don't forget your family.

APRIL

Find the Gold in the Grind in April: A coach must know his own strengths and weaknesses as well as his players'. He must know how to increase and develop strengths and how to compensate and improve weaknesses. It is not easy becoming a coach, and anyone who thinks it is is only fooling themselves. Prepare for the grind of the post-season.

Remember: to get full value, take notes each day. Use the note-taking section after each nugget or have your "Nugget Notebook" at your side.

April 1

The Practice
One player who believes he can win is worth a team full of players who only think they can.

The Game
You must believe deeply that you can get better, that you can win; and that spirit will transcend all those around you. Be contagious: spread your convictions.

Word Thought
TRANSCEND

*Notes*_____

_____

_____

April 2

The Practice

"Nothing splendid has ever been achieved except by those who dared believe that something inside them was superior to circumstances."
– Bruce Barton

The Game

To be a basketball coach or player is a great challenge. They have an inner calling that draws them toward the grind and the risk. It's not really an ego thing; it's an attraction to the spirit of the game: to feel that which not everyone feels, whether in victory or defeat, success or failure.

Word Thought
CALLING

*Notes*_____

_____

_____

April 3

The Practice

Great shooters know before they receive the pass if they will have an open shot or not.

The Game

The great shooters in the game anticipate when they are going to be open and don't react when they come open. They have a feel for space on the floor, the quickness of the defenders, the teammate delivering the ball, that allows them to know if they will get an open shot or if they will use a dribble. Awareness gets you shot opportunities.

Word Thought
AWARENESS

*Notes*_____

_____

_____

April 4

The Practice

They say that basketball is a game of inches and that Larry Bird and Reggie Miller were the masters of the half inch.

The Game

These were two of the greatest at moving without the ball and reading screens. Their mastery was their ability to gain just a half inch advantage off a screen to create a shot. Not two of the quickest players to play but definitely two of the most aware.

Word Thought

ADVANTAGE

*Notes*_____

_____

_____

April 5

The Practice

Shared suffering: One guy messes up and everyone runs. Shared pleasure: One guy does well and the whole team benefits.

The Game

Many players have difficulty understanding this concept. They ask, "Why should I suffer consequences for someone else's mistake?" Great teams and great players thoroughly understand the value of this concept. Accountability and putting the needs of others ahead of oneself push teams above and beyond their physical limitations.

Word Thought

ACCOUNTABILITY

*Notes*_____

_____

_____

April 6

The Practice
It's not what you tell players. It's what they hear.

The Game
If gathering knowledge is vital to success as a player, then listening skills are a key way to gather. Do you really listen to the coaching or do you hear it? Tuning into your coach's message and not the circumstances around why he is delivering it is the key.

Word Thought
LISTENING

*Notes*_____

_____

_____

April 7

The Practice
Basketball is a game of habits.

The Game
We all have good habits and bad habits. The pressure of the game will cause you to draw upon only the most ingrained skills and responses (habits). You must break old bad habits by replacing them with good habits and solidify those good habits so they emerge during the pressure of the game. Remember, you become your habits in pressure situations. This is true for coaches too.

Word Thought
HABITS

*Notes*_____

_____

_____

April 8

The Practice

The happiest coaches are those who have harvested their time in others. The unhappiest coaches are those who wonder how the game is going to make them happy.

– John C. Maxwell (paraphrase)

The Game

There are givers and takers in this world. Sometimes it seems as though there are a lot more takers. Learn the real joy of being a giver and seeing someone benefit from your guidance and leadership. Give to a cause greater than yourself.

Word Thought

GIVERS

*Notes*_____

_____

_____

April 9

The Practice

The 'big time' is not a place, it's the state of your heart. It's not something you get but something you become.

The Game

Everybody wants to be in the big time. Every coach wants to get to the NCAA finals. This mindset often is counter-productive to individual and team performance. Be the best you can be. Make your place at an institution or in a program the best it can be. Learn to help others through the position you have and where you have it.

Word Thought

COUNTER-PRODUCTIVE

*Notes*_____

_____

_____

April 10

The Practice

The most important individual defensive fundamental is the 'close out.' This must be practiced daily.

The Game

The transition from helping a teammate to recovering to your own man is a time of great vulnerability for any defensive player. Proper technique – body angle, hand position, weight distribution, knowledge of player being guarded – is necessary to be able to defend. Gather the knowledge.

Word Thought

TECHNIQUE

*Notes*_____

_____

_____

April 11

The Practice

Defense and rebounding are a matter of hustle, desire and pride more than anything else.

– Tex Winter

The Game

You can take a player who can't jump over the lines on the floor and they can become a leading defender and rebounder. It is a mindset, a focus that sets those players apart. You have to truly see the value in that role and savor the effort it requires.

Word Thought

MINDSET

*Notes*_____

_____

_____

April 12

The Practice

No amount of preparation is too much for a determined coach and player and team.

The Game

The lights go on. The band is playing. The national anthem has been sung. the game is about to begin. But the contest has already been decided. The preparation, hard work, dedication, countless hours on the floor and off the floor, out of sight of all the spectators, has already determined the victor in the game and in life.

Don't wait for the opening tipoff – work hard every day.

Word Thought
DECIDED

*Notes*_____

_____

_____

April 13

The Practice

There are some pigs in this world. Remember this rule: "Don't ever wrestle with a pig. You both get dirty and the pig likes it."
– Attributed to George Bernard Shaw

The Game

Coaches must deal with negative, even jealous people who love to find the flaw or weak spot of others. Guard yourself when with these people. Be pleasant and respectful, never phony. But watch what you say and how you say it. It could come back to haunt you.

Word Thought
PHONY

*Notes*_____

_____

_____

WOODY HAYES WEEK
April 14 – 20

Woody Hayes became a mentor of mine after I took one of his classes, "The Theory of Coaching Football," while I was pursuing my master's degree at Ohio State. He taught about blocking and tackling, offensive and defensive schemes, the importance of specialty teams, but mostly he taught about life. How to build and maintain relationships, how to motivate his staff and the players. He talked about not letting the game tear you down. He was a great teacher and a revered mentor of mine. Even though he crossed the line (we all know about the slap) he is, in my eyes, one of the great coaches in the history of the game.

Dance on the edge, but be careful you don't slip. Have a great week with Woody.

Woody Hayes Week   **April 14**

The Practice
"You win with people."
– Wayne Woodrow "Woody" Hayes

The Game
You really win with great players who work hard and who are talented. Then you mold the players into becoming the best they can become. You must communicate and relate well to the players and also your assistants, the parents, your administration, the officials, the media and the fans. Remember this: you may have all the X's and O's knowledge in the world, but if you don't know how to work well with people you won't get the wins.

Word Thought
PEOPLE

*Notes*_____

_____

_____

Woody Hayes Week   April 15

The Practice

"I will pound you and pound you until you quit."
– Coach Woody Hayes

The Game

Don't you just love the old guys? He didn't just mean 'on the field', but in the classroom and even in your social life. He wanted to pound you to become the best. What a challenge!

Word Thought

POUND

*Notes*_____

_____

_____

Woody Hayes Week   April 16

The Practice

"There's nothing that cleanses your soul like getting the hell kicked out of you!"
– Coach Woody Hayes

The Game

If you coach long enough, this will certainly happen. When I coached basketball, one night we were on the road and we were behind 27 to 6 at the half. I walked across the floor and asked the rowdy football team of our opponents who were on the bleachers if they would cheer for me in the second half. They agreed to. I then went to my team and said, "If we lose by more than 20 we will stay here and practice." We lost by 19. I got a standing ovation at the end of the game from the fans of the opposing team. This really cleansed my soul.

Word Thought

CLEANSE

*Notes*_____

_____

_____

Woody Hayes Week April 17

The Practice
"I don't apologize for anything. When I make a mistake, I take the blame and go on from there."
– Coach Woody Hayes

The Game
As a coach, I have apologized for my actions, but have seldom blamed the players, the other coaches or the officials. Accept, evaluate (this is essential), learn and get on with it.

Word Thought
APOLOGIZE

*Notes*_____

_____

_____

Woody Hayes Week April 18

The Practice
"I may not be able to outsmart too many people, but I can outwork 'em."
– Coach Woody Hayes

The Game
Attention to details, willingness to go over things one more time, staying in the office overnight, coming back to the office early after a road loss can make you look a lot smarter then you might be – and be a lot more successful.

Word Thought
OUTSMART

*Notes*_____

_____

_____

Woody Hayes Week | April 19

The Practice
"I may not be very smart, but I recognize that I am not very smart."
– Coach Woody Hayes

The Game
Most of us think sometimes we are better than we are. Some players think they are better players than they are. One of the great secrets in coaching is to become aware of your strengths and weaknesses and make the players aware of theirs. Knowing who you are is real smart.

Word Thought
SMART

*Notes*_____

_____

_____

Woody Hayes Week | April 20

The Practice
"Success is what you do with what you got."
– Coach Woody Hayes

The Game
There is nothing here about winning and losing, yet we all know how badly Woody always wanted to win. This is about doing the best every day with what you have where you are. Be the best coach where you are today.

Word Thought
SUCCESS

*Notes*_____

_____

_____

April 21

The Practice

"Sometimes a player's greatest challenge is coming to grips with his role on the team."

– Scottie Pippen

The Game

Scottie Pippen has the NBA championship rings to show for this quote. He's a man who in his own right was a fabulous player, perhaps the second best player of the entire era. He could have had a scoring title, he could have been a hero in many places, but he wanted to win championships. So he accepted the role of playing second fiddle to a guy named Jordan, and that became his claim to fame. Learning to accept roles for the good of the team may be the single most important issue to be cleared before a team can grow.

Word Thought

ROLE

*Notes*_____

_____

_____

April 22

The Practice

We must practice to become better, not just to win the game.

The Game

Let winning be a by-product of the effort, intensity and attitude you have toward practice.

Word Thought

BY-PRODUCT

*Notes*_____

_____

_____

April 23

The Practice

To win a hundred games out of a hundred is not the highest joy, but to win the hearts of all the friends and enemies you made while winning – **there** is real joy.

The Game

Winning is fun. It's a great thing to want to win the game. However, you must never lose sight of how important relationships with people are.

Word Thought

RELATIONSHIPS

*Notes*_____

_____

_____

April 24

The Practice

To know you can't shoot the ball is the beginning of wisdom.

The Game

Being able to evaluate your skills and play to your strengths and weaknesses is the sign of a true team player.

Word Thought

WISDOM

*Notes*_____

_____

_____

April 25

The Practice

Those who are aware that our coaching will soon come to an end will quit their quarreling with referees at once.

The Game

Things look so much different at the end of practice, or the game, or the season, or a career. Be sure you don't have any regrets.

Word Thought

REGRETS

*Notes*_____

_____

_____

April 26

The Practice

When one eye is constantly fixed on winning, there is only one eye left with which to find the best way.

– Zen saying (paraphrase)

The Game

You must keep both eyes on the task at hand. The important thing is to practice hard and then let whatever happens, happen.

Word Thought

EYES

*Notes*_____

_____

_____

April 27

The Practice

Great players say, "I will get it done." Poor players have only wishes.

The Game

To become a great player you must work hard, put in the time and develop great habits. You must decide to do this regardless of the time and effort.

Word Thought

WISHES

*Notes*_____

_____

_____

April 28

The Practice

You must pay an extra price every day in practice to be better than the other teams.

The Game

It's easy to let up on the players in practice, particularly when you're winning. But remember that the other teams are practicing hard, and when you meet, guess who will win!

Word Thought

PRICE

*Notes*_____

_____

_____

April 29

The Practice

It is better to aim a little high on your shots and hope it bounces in than to never get your shots to the rim.

The Game

You must set your goals high – even if you miss, you achieve much – rather than setting your goals too low and reaching them, but not achieving much.

Word Thought

AIM

*Notes*_____

_____

_____

April 30

The Practice

"Use the past as a springboard, not a sofa."
– Harold Macmillan

The Game

To put it another way, use the past as a springboard to leap over obstacles. You can't rely on what has happened before and can't afford to take it easy because of past successes.

Word Thought

SUCCESSES

*Notes*_____

_____

_____

Re-read the introduction to the Post-Season.

MAY

Find the Gold in the Grind in May: *Today's culture won't let you coach the "my way or the highway" philosophy. To get the best out of your players, you need to work with them and empower them and yourself! They must develop intrinsic motivation for the off-season.* The Daily Nugget *is designed to help you do just that.*

Remember: to get full value, take notes each day. Use the note-taking section after each nugget or have your "Nugget Notebook" at your side.

May 1

The Practice
Don't just be good, be as good as possible. Remember, good can be the enemy of best.

The Game
To excel you must be better than good. Don't ever be satisfied with where you are. Always strive for better and best.

Word Thought
EXCEL

*Notes*_____

_____

_____

May 2

The Practice

"The masters all have the ability to discipline themselves to eliminate everything except what they are trying to accomplish."
– Coach Dale Brown

The Game

In coaching and in all areas of your life, time management is vital. Success requires having a plan and the ability to focus on details. You must concentrate your energies on the task at hand and not allow other areas to drift into your thoughts. Stay on task and maintain balance among your tasks.

Word Thought

FOCUS

*Notes*_____

_____

_____

May 3

The Practice

"What you get by reaching your goals is not nearly as important as what you become by reaching them."
– Hilary Hinton "Zig" Ziglar

The Game

The real goal is to develop great young people who grow and become solid, caring adults. Water with care now, watch them grow later.

Word Thought

DEVELOP

*Notes*_____

_____

_____

May 4

The Practice
The coach cannot always be interested in the reasons you didn't practice well. He only wants to know what will make you better.

The Game
Coaches are a lot alike. They don't want excuses, they just want you to show them how much you care about the team and about getting better.

Word Thought
EXCUSES

*Notes*_____

_____

_____

May 5

The Practice
If you want to improve, you must gradually develop the habit of always wanting to get better.

The Game
You must do the little things every day in the right way and little by little you will become a lot better.

Word Thought
GRADUALLY

*Notes*_____

_____

_____

May 6

The Practice
The higher a player jumps, the more his rear is exposed.

The Game
The more exposed you are, the more pressure is exposed. Tug up your pants, cover the cracks in your game, and leap ahead.

Word Thought
EXPOSED

*Notes*_____

_____

_____

May 7

The Practice
Be able to assess the talents you have and make the most of them.

The Game
This is true for the coach and player. To know thyself is important. To know yourself isn't a little thing – it's everything.

Word Thought
ASSESS

*Notes*_____

_____

_____

May 8

The Practice

Self-control may be the foundation for excellence in coaching and in playing.

The Game

You must discipline yourself in tough practices and in tough times. You must not retreat or give in to your emotions. Excellence doesn't just show up. It is formed day in and day out by self-control.

Word Thought

SELF-CONTROL

*Notes*_____

_____

_____

May 9

The Practice

No amount of practice and no amount of coaching will help you if you believe someone else is responsible for your improvement.

The Game

You must take action and do what is necessary to make yourself better. Sure, a good coach or teacher can help; sure, teammates are a positive asset; but in the end they can do nothing if you don't first step up to the foul line. In the end it is up to you.

Word Thought

RESPONSIBILITY

*Notes*_____

_____

_____

May 10

The Practice

Everyone wants to excel, but to be really excellent you must develop proper habits.

The Game

One of the first things you must do is to develop proper work habits. The ability to stick to something when it gets difficult comes from doing it over and over. You develop the habit of not giving up or giving in. *"Do it 4,999 times and then once more!"*
– Dr. Forrest Clare "Phog" Allen

Word Thought

PROPER

*Notes*_____

_____

_____

May 11

The Practice

Let others want to teach and coach by watching me.

The Game

Coaching and teaching are honorable professions. Having a role model is important for every student-athlete. They reflect the teacher-coach in their lives. Be worthy of that reflection.

Word Thought

ROLE MODEL

*Notes*_____

_____

_____

May 12

The Practice
We cannot look directly into the hearts of players, but their actions during practice are open for observation.

The Game
The ability to evaluate accurately is a key to being a good coach. Looking at the total person – not just the body, but also the heart and mind – is essential.

Word Thought
EVALUATE

*Notes*_____

_____

_____

May 13

The Practice
Have an absolutely clear vision of the goals and unity of the team. Pursue it with a passion – practice is not supposed to be easy.

The Game
You must be clear about what you want to accomplish each day. Team unity must be a high priority. Make the tough practices as enjoyable as you can but work them hard.

Word Thought
VISION

*Notes*_____

_____

_____

MICHAEL JORDAN WEEK
May 14 – 20

Michael Jordan is thought by many to be the greatest player of all time. He took his game mentally and physically to its highest level. I am certain no one was ever better mentally. He was knowledgeable, he was tough mentally, he was the best late in the game. He was one that anyone would want to coach. Enjoy your week's engagement with Michael Jordan!

Michael Jordan Week   May 14

The Practice
"I always had the ultimate goal of being the best. But I approached everything step by step, setting short-term goals."
– Michael Jordan

The Game
Having clear, concise goals and objectives is a must for any player or coach at any level. You can't make great leaps, you must take tiny steps.

Word Thought
ACHIEVEMENT

*Notes*_____
_____
_____

Michael Jordan Week   May 15

The Practice

"If it turns out my best isn't good enough then at least I'll never be able to look back and say I was too afraid to try."
– Michael Jordan

The Game

You can't be afraid of failure. You must give it a try. The only true failure is not trying or not getting back up once you fail. Remember, Michael Jordan was cut as a high school sophomore.

Word Thought

AFRAID

*Notes*_____

_____

_____

Michael Jordan Week   May 16

The Practice

"You have to monitor your fundamentals constantly, because the only thing that changes will be your attention to them. The fundamentals never change."
– Michael Jordan

The Game

It is up to the coaches to present solid fundamentals in practice and up to the players to understand and appreciate the value of each drill. One of Michael's strengths was his mental talent and ability to always go back to fundamentals.

Word Thought

CONSTANTLY

*Notes*_____

_____

_____

Michael Jordan Week   May 17

The Practice

"I've always tried to lead by example, never by talking, because words never mean as much as action."

– Michael Jordan

The Game

You must prove yourself every day in practice. We all like to say how good we are. Don't tell me, show me, every day.

Word Thought

EXAMPLE

Notes_____

_____

_____

Michael Jordan Week   May 18

The Practice

"You aren't the leader because you are the best player on the team; you have to gain the respect of those around you by your actions."

– Michael Jordan

The Game

You may not be the biggest, have the great hops, or rainbow the threes when it counts, but you can practice at a level that gains the respect of your teammates and will make you a leader on the team and in life.

Word Thought

RESPECT

Notes_____

_____

_____

Michael Jordan Week   May 19

The Practice

"You don't have to play a professional sport to be an effective leader. Every home, every business, every neighborhood and every family needs someone to lead."

– Michael Jordan

The Game

Developing leadership skills should be a goal every day in every practice for every person. Transference of skills, attitudes, and values that develop leadership is important on the floor and off the floor.

Word Thought

TRANSFERENCE

Notes _____

_____

_____

Michael Jordan Week   May 20

The Practice

"I can accept failure. Everyone fails at something. But I can't accept not trying."

– Michael Jordan

The Game

In sports, particularly basketball, you will face defeat or failure in many ways. Losing is an obvious way, but also not making a team, not starting, or not being the leading scorer. Look at failures as opportunities in disguise, opportunities to learn and improve. Once you have learned the lesson of a failure you will be much better. Never stop trying.

Word Thought

FAILURE

Notes _____

_____

_____

May 21

The Practice

Here are four things to give your players:
1. The best knowledge of the game
2. A good role model
3. All the love you can
4. Trust

The Game

Give freely and willingly. Time is also important to give, but you can't beat the four statements above.

Word Thought

GIVE

*Notes*_____

_____

_____

May 22

The Practice

The longer you coach, the more you need to adjust to changing times, and yet you must cling to unchanging principles.

– Julia Coleman (paraphrase)

The Game

There will be a constant battle to do things the way you've always done them or to change to new ideas and techniques. Adjust, but keep what you value most.

Word Thought

ADJUST

*Notes*_____

_____

_____

May 23

The Practice

Playing the game always involves risk. You can't steal the ball with your hands behind your back.

The Game

You must be willing to gamble and risk without jeopardizing everything. Take chances but be smart in the way you attempt to steal the ball.

Word Thought

RISK

*Notes*_____

_____

_____

May 24

The Practice

"It is not the critic who counts; not the man who points out how the strong man stumbles, or where the doer of deeds could have done better. The credit belongs to the man who is actually in the arena."
– Theodore Roosevelt

The Game

Spend your time coaching young people. Take the risk of leading your team, even risk your job, in making the team better **your** way. What a great opportunity to practice, to play, to work hard, maybe to fail. It is far greater than never to attempt.

Word Thought

CRITICISM

*Notes*_____

_____

_____

May 25

The Practice

One of the first secrets of success is to trust yourself. Then you can trust others.

The Game

You must believe in yourself. Game and hard work can help you build that confidence so you can be an important part of a team.

Word Thought

TRUST

*Notes*_____

_____

_____

May 26

The Practice

No team can succeed until it learns that playing defense is as exciting and satisfying as playing offense.

The Game

You must have balance as a player and a team. Be willing to work hard at both ends of the floor and enjoy the trip up and down.

Word Thought

BALANCE

*Notes*_____

_____

_____

May 27

The Practice

The game is neither good nor bad, a lot of fun or a pain. It is what you make it. The choice is yours.

The Game

Your attitude will determine your altitude. We've all heard that. It's true that you get to decide how you respond to practice and to life. You can't control the length of practice but you can control how hard you play.

Word Thought

DECIDE

*Notes*_____

_____

_____

May 28

The Practice

Learn from the mistakes of others. The season isn't long enough to make them all yourself.

The Game

In the game or in practice you must constantly be watching others when they do great things and watching when they make turnovers. You can learn in every type of situation.

Word Thought

WATCH

*Notes*_____

_____

_____

May 29

The Practice

We know nothing about tomorrow's practice. The goal should be to practice as hard and as good as you can today. Stay in the moment. That's the best preparation for tomorrow.

The Game

It is difficult indeed not to think ahead, to worry about what is next. In a way, that is not all bad. But to stay in the moment and to work hard today will make all your tomorrows better.

Word Thought

TOMORROW

*Notes*_____

_____

_____

May 30

The Practice

It's not about having great talent but in developing to its fullest the talent you are blessed with.

The Game

The real victories lie in doing the very best you can, in working and striving and practicing each day to become the best you are capable of becoming.

Word Thought

BECOMING

*Notes*_____

_____

_____

May 31

The Practice

A foolish player can't wait for the practice to end. The wise player knows that there is no end to practice.

The Game

You must be able to see the entire situation. A lot of bad players are done with practice before it's over. They just go through the motions and it seems like it's never going to end. Shorten your practice by giving all you've got every second.

Word Thought

PRACTICE

*Notes*_____

_____

_____

Re-read the introduction to the Post-Season.

Post-Season Summary

Review your notes from the Post-Season and reflect on the events and insights that have taken place. Write down your answers to the following three questions on the lines below or in your "Nugget Notebook."

What did you learn from the Post-Season Daily Nuggets?

_____

_____

_____

Are you ready for the Summer Season?

_____

_____

_____

Which Word Thought was most important for you and why? Keep using that word going forward.

_____

_____

_____

SUMMER SEASON

June – July – August

There is no off-season. There is only a short bounce pass from one stage to the next. You've got to continue motivating yourself and your players every day!

"Just do it!" Every day.

In order to do that, you'll need to maintain contact with your players throughout the summer, even though everyone (except a few Division I teams) scatters for jobs, internships, vacations and family time.

How do you combat this separation? How can you maintain contact with your players without being intrusive or suffocating? Some time off is a good thing for the players and for the coach: everyone needs some separation, some time away from the demands of the coach.

This is a time for encouragement and lifting, for supporting and deepening relationships that strengthen the team. That's easier when everybody is reading the same thing and thinking about the same topics and sharing their ideas. Each person thinks his own thoughts, but we are all focused on the same topic. This is deeply important and that's where *The Daily Nugget* will be invaluable.

You must have a plan to develop relationships. Keep coaching – keep caring – keep communicating. Build those relationships that bind the team together.

JUNE

Find the Gold in the Grind in June: *You want to be a great coach? Then be a lifter and developer of wonderful young men and women by studying and engaging* The Daily Nugget. *Establish an atmosphere of trust and caring, and develop relationships. The summer is a great time to make changes and adjustments.*

Remember: to get full value, take notes each day. Use the note-taking section after each nugget or have your "Nugget Notebook" at your side.

June 1

The Practice
"Very little is needed to make a happy life; it is all within yourself, within your way of thinking."
– Marcus Aurelius

The Game
You cannot control all situations and circumstances in life, but you can control how you respond. Being positive and uplifting can truly make your team better.

Word Thought
CONTROL

*Notes*_____
_____
_____

June 2

The Practice

When you put on your practice gear, be sure and lace up a great attitude, even in the summer time.

The Game

Be sure and work on your mental frame of mind every day. One of the most important things you can wear is a wonderful expression and smile.

Word Thought

EXPRESSION

*Notes*_____

_____

_____

June 3

The Practice

Everyone wants a stronger team and people are lifting more weight and at a younger age. If you really want a strong team, lift each other with positive attitudes.

The Game

There are a lot of ways to get better, including working on fundamentals and lifting weights. Be a lifter of weights and a lifter of hearts as well.

Word Thought

LIFT

*Notes*_____

_____

_____

June 4

The Practice

Gratitude can hold a team together. Rally your team with gratitude if it begins to fall apart.

The Game

By showing that you care, that you are grateful for the effort that has been given, you can rally a team to new heights.

Word Thought

GRATITUDE

*Notes*_____

_____

_____

June 5

The Practice

Coaches must expect from others only what they expect of themselves.

The Game

You must be a role model of expectation. Demand and expect from those around you only what you demand and expect of yourself.

Word Thought

EXPECTATION

*Notes*_____

_____

_____

June 6

The Practice

The only way to have great teammates is to be one.

The Game

You must be the example of a great teammate, willing to give up yourself for the good of the team. Be a good teammate yourself, and you will have good teammates.

Word Thought

TEAMMATE

*Notes*_____

_____

_____

June 7

The Practice

Everybody involved – coaches, players, parents, officials, administrators, fans – all need to be kind to each other, for in their own way everybody feels the stress.

The Game

Everybody has battles to fight and it is tough at times. By being kind and supportive, you lift yourself and all those around you.

Word Thought

KIND

*Notes*_____

_____

_____

June 8

The Practice
There's great joy in knowing that the more we give and the more we share, the more we get and the more we receive.

The Game
It's easy to be selfish, to want things for ourselves, but the really great players and teams understand that giving is the true victory in the game of life. *"Giving gets."*
– *The Golden Whistle,* Golden Nugget No. 2, "You Become Your Habits in Pressure Situations"

Word Thought
GIVE

*Notes*_____

_____

_____

June 9

The Practice
Always do more than the coach or teacher expects of you. Hold yourself to a higher standard and never make excuses.

The Game
Always doing more will not guarantee you will win the game, but you will always win in life. Doing more is a habit you can develop.

Word Thought
EXCUSES

*Notes*_____

_____

_____

CLASS AND CHARACTER WEEK
June 10 – 17

You want to win so bad when you are young that it can blind you to the reality of your situation. Class and character are easy to talk about and easy to expound upon until the pressure puts you up to your ass in alligators. You will eventually handle the game better. In the meantime, you may need to search for a mentor to keep you on track.

During your discussions, be sure to put each Word Thought within the context of Class and Character.

Have a great week.

Note: Class and character are so essential that I've made this an eight-day week, like a baker's dozen, except in basketball you have so much to do that you often wish for an extra day. Here it is!

Class and Character Week　　　　　　　　June 10

The Practice
"Fame is a vapor, popularity an accident, riches take wings. Only one thing endures – character."
– Horace Greeley

The Game
People may forget your record, but they will always remember the way you treated them. If you make people feel good about themselves, they will treat you with class. Go to the hoop, young man, go to the hoop!

Word Thought
CHARACTER

*Notes*_____
_____
_____

Class and Character Week   **June 11**

The Practice

Class is respect for others. It is a deep and genuine respect for every player regardless of status on the team.

The Game

You must care and respect yourself and then you can share it with others. Make everyone around you feel better by demonstrating self-respect, showing respect to others and sharing your love.

Word Thought

CLASS

*Notes*_____

_____

_____

Class and Character Week   **June 12**

The Practice

Class is having manners. It is always saying, "Thank you" and 'Please." It is complimenting other coaches, players, parents, and officials for any and every task that was done well.

The Game

In the heat of practice or the game, it is often difficult to behave in a positive way. If the coach sets the way, it becomes easier for everyone involved.

Word Thought

MANNERS

*Notes*_____

_____

_____

Class and Character Week   June 13

The Practice

Having character is treating other coaches, players, and all involved as you would want them to treat you during practices and games.

The Game

This version of the Golden Rule, "Do unto others," certainly applies every day at practice, at every game, and to all people involved. Character and respect are like gold in any relationship.

Word Thought

TREAT

*Notes*_____

_____

_____

Class and Character Week   June 14

The Practice

Class never makes excuses for the players' or team's or coach's shortcomings and it will help all to bounce back from their mistakes.

The Game

There are circumstances that make us want to blame others, but class will allow us to be a lifter at that moment and help all those around us to feel better fast.

Word Thought

EXCUSES

*Notes*_____

_____

_____

Class and Character Week June 15

The Practice

Class never brags or boasts in victory and never tears down or diminishes the achievements of opponents when you have been defeated.

The Game

Keep your pride under control in victory and be gallant in defeat. Wow. These are difficult challenges, but worth the effort. Being competitive and under pressure to win makes this really challenging. Accept the challenge!

Word Thought

BRAG

*Notes*_____

_____

_____

Class and Character Week June 16

The Practice

Class means you don't select a team on the basis of money, family, connections, status or success.

The Game

It might be easy to select players based on these types of things, but you must be careful and do what is right.

Word Thought

SELECT

*Notes*_____

_____

_____

The Practice

If you and your team have character, everyone will see it and know it. If you are without character – good luck, because no matter what you accomplish it will never have meaning.

The Game

Character will show. George Bernard Shaw once said, *"People are always blaming their circumstances for what they are. I don't believe in circumstances. People with character are the ones who get up and look for the circumstances they want and, if they can't find them, make them."* Game character makes you classy.

Word Thought

BELIEVE

*Notes*_____

_____

_____

June 18

The Practice

When you are angry, moderation is a virtue. When you are defending your principles, moderation is a vice.
– Thomas Paine (paraphrase)

The Game

Standing firm in your beliefs and principles is an important part of coaching and teaching. Being able to control your anger is a gift that will continue to give back to you the rest of your life.

Word Thought

MODERATION

*Notes*_____

_____

_____

June 19

The Practice

Nothing is lacking more in today's practices than the powerful combination of hard work towards the goal of getting better and the ability to embrace the present moment.

The Game

Working hard is not the total answer. Working smart is imperative, along with the ability to concentrate and stay in the moment.

Word Thought

EMBRACE

*Notes*_____

_____

_____

June 20

The Practice

Concentration is a learned behavior. It doesn't happen automatically. You must establish easy, repeatable, progressive routines that you can then depend on during the pressure of the game.

The Game

The ability to stay in the moment - mindfulness - is a skill like shooting or ball handling that can be developed and improved. And it's just as important. To be able to concentrate under great pressure should be a goal of all coaches and teachers for themselves and for their players.

Word Thought

CONCENTRATION

*Notes*_____

_____

_____

June 21

The Practice
Picture yourself doing things correctly.

The Game
The mind cannot tell the difference between a real experience and a mental experience. This is true in practice and in games. You must be able to see your team winning, to see each shot going in. The subconscious mind will react to whatever you put in it. Go positive.

Word Thought
SUBCONSCIOUS

*Notes*_____

_____

_____

June 22

The Practice
It is good to teach problem-solving and decision-making skills in practice.

The Game
As a coach or teacher, you should be trying to develop fundamentals of the game. But, by also teaching cognitive (mental) skills such as problem-solving and decision-making, you are teaching skills that will enhance your players for their lifetimes.

Word Thought
DECISIONS

*Notes*_____

_____

_____

June 23

The Practice
There is a fine line between a sense of urgency – "we have a lot that we need to work on" – and a sense of panic – "there isn't enough time to get everything in."

The Game
There is always an uncomfortable feeling when the practices get closer to the games. If you hold well-organized practices that allow learning through progression of skills, you will lessen the sense of panic on game days.

Word Thought
ORGANIZE

*Notes*_____

_____

_____

June 24

The Practice
If you have excitement for the game, you should thank God for that. If you don't, you should get down on your knees and pray for it.

The Game
The coach and the players must be ready to practice with a great deal of enthusiasm every day, then you will play that way on game day.

Word Thought
ENTHUSIASM

*Notes*_____

_____

_____

June 25

The Practice

When dealing with parents, don't stir muddy waters.

The Game

Being able to anticipate problems or situations you may find yourself in will help you handle these situations better. Reacting in a calm, positive way is really important.

Word Thought

ANTICIPATE

*Notes*_____

_____

_____

June 26

The Practice

How long would you coach if you didn't know how long you have already coached?

The Game

How long would you work, practice or play if you didn't know? You, of course, will know and you must continue to work hard. This takes real mental toughness.

Word Thought

PERSISTENCE

*Notes*_____

_____

_____

June 27

The Practice

No matter how well you practice you can always practice better. That's the fun of it.

The Game

What makes a great player number one in the world? It goes beyond talent to the discipline it takes to practice hard and practice smart.

Word Thought

PRACTICE

*Notes*_____

_____

_____

June 28

The Practice

Understanding the game is the path to winning, and not knowing is the path to losing. Those who understand do not lose, but those who do not know are already headed toward losing.

The Game

You must understand the game, the people, the circumstances that surround you. You can never know too much. Keep striving to learn and understand the game.

Word Thought

UNDERSTANDING

*Notes*_____

_____

_____

June 29

The Practice

Which is better – the one who knows what to do or the one who loves to do it?

The Game

Of course, the answer is both. You must know what to do and then be motivated to do it. Don't tell me you know, show me.

Word Thought

SHOW

*Notes*_____

_____

_____

June 30

The Practice

The superior player seeks what is best for the team. The inferior player, what is best for me.

The Game

The great players can put their ego aside and play for the team. This is a trait that comes naturally, but can be improved with practice and hard work.

Word Thought

TEAMWORK

*Notes*_____

_____

_____

Re-read the introduction to the Summer Season.

JULY

Find the Gold in the Grind in July: I hope this book helps you no matter where you are on your coaching and life journeys. You must dig for the nuggets. They will probably not drop out of the sky into your lap.

Remember: to get full value, take notes each day. Use the note-taking section after each nugget or have your "Nugget Notebook" at your side.

July 1

The Practice
In order for a game to be capable of being won, it must also be capable of being lost.

The Game
You cannot fear losing or playing poorly. You must practice and prepare the best you can and let the ball bounce the way it will.

Word Thought
CHANCE

Notes_____

_____

_____

July 2

The Practice
The player who is consistent in his practice effort is the most valuable player.

The Game
People will rally behind you if you are consistent on every drill in every day.

Word Thought
CONSISTENT

*Notes*_____

_____

_____

July 3

The Practice
If you want to be in great condition for the games, then practice hard every day. Push yourself for peak conditioning.

The Game
We say it time after time: you must push yourself to reach peak condition. No coach can make you do it. No player can do it for you. You must lay it on the line every day yourself.

Word Thought
GREATNESS

*Notes*_____

_____

_____

July 4

The Practice

Being a lifter in practice, working hard in every drill and being excited in all circumstances are what make winners and leaders.

The Game

There is a certain glow in players who give it all every day. You can see it in their faces – the grin, the energy, the pure joy of practice.

Word Thought

ENERGY

*Notes*_____

_____

_____

July 5

The Practice

Many players hesitate at the most difficult moments in practice. They also find themselves hesitating on the threshold of victory in the big games.

The Game

You must give your best all the time. You cannot doubt yourself or hesitate at those difficult moments. A lot of players are so close and never quite get it done.

Word Thought

HESITATE

*Notes*_____

_____

_____

July 6

The Practice

Everyone says it's good to play hard. That's true, but you must also have mastery over your passions.

The Game

You must have great excitement and yet, at the same time, execute great control to be able to totally develop all your talents. Reacting to difficult situations is good, but to what degree can make all the difference.

Word Thought
MASTERY

*Notes*_____

_____

_____

July 7

The Practice

If the only thing you ever say to your coach or parent is "Thank you," it will be enough.

The Game

No matter what the practices were like or how the season went with wins or losses, the ability to say "Thank you" can mean so much to so many. My own greatest moment in sports was on Senior Night at Ohio State University with my son, Jay. I was in tears because it was all over. Jay came back across the floor of St. John's Arena, put his arm around my shoulders and said, "Thank you, Dad. If it weren't for you I would never have played for Ohio State."

Word Thought
THANK YOU

*Notes*_____

_____

_____

July 8

The Practice

If you can be pushed hard in practice and be grateful for the experience, you are special indeed.

The Game

Finding joy in whatever experience you find yourself in in life is a gift you can give yourself that's more valuable than gold.

Word Thought

EXPERIENCE

*Notes*_____

_____

_____

July 9

The Practice

Cherish the moments you have in practice and games, with the players and parents, officials and administrators. It all ends too soon.

The Game

Capturing the moment and enjoying each experience is difficult to do in coaching with all its related stress and pressure. But it is worth trying as much as possible because it helps you get better.

Word Thought

CHERISH

*Notes*_____

_____

_____

July 10

The Practice

It's a rare coach or player who can enjoy every moment of every practice or game, but striving for this is a joy in itself.

The Game

Don't we love to be around those people who seem to be able to enjoy even the most difficult moments? Seek these people out, try to emulate them, and your life will be better.

Word Thought

EMULATE

*Notes*_____

_____

_____

July 11

The Practice

Be quick to praise and slow to criticize.

The Game

Be aware of how hurtful words can be. If you do criticize someone once in awhile, make sure you are also prepared to love them all the time, and to show that love.

Word Thought

CRITICIZE

*Notes*_____

_____

_____

OLD-TIMERS FOOTBALL COACHES WEEK
July 12 – 18

I played college football and taught it at the high school and college level, so my first real association with coaching and coaching clinics was through football. I love all coaches, but found that the older football coaches were really a tough, smart breed. They may not fit in today, but there's true wisdom in much of what they say.

Listen, appreciate and adapt where it can be valuable. My college coach, Ed Sherman, and Woody Hayes were good coaching buddies. Both had solid coaching and teaching philosophies that I still admire today.

Old-Timers Football Coaches Week   July 12

The Practice
"Build for your team a feeling of oneness, of dependence on one another and of strength to be derived by unity."
– Coach Vince Lombardi

The Game
In basketball, all players perform all skills of the game. Look at your own team. Do you look beyond your own position? Do you understand the overall process and how your job fits into something larger? Do you see how interdependent you are?

Word Thought
DEPENDENCE

*Notes*_____

_____

_____

Old-Timers Football Coaches Week   July 13

The Practice

"Don't forget your fundamentals – fundamentals in the game and fundamentals in life."

– Coach Tony Dungy

The Game

You must practice basketball every day, but also keep in mind your family, friends and academics need you too.

Word Thought

FUNDAMENTALS

*Notes*_____

_____

_____

Old-Timers Football Coaches Week   July 14

The Practice

"There is a misconception about teamwork. Teamwork is the ability to have different thoughts about things; it's the ability to argue and stand up and say loud and strong what you feel. But in the end, it's also the ability to adjust to what is best for the team."

– Coach Tom Landry

The Game

Being part of the team doesn't mean you give up being an individual or expressing yourself on and off the court. What it does mean is that when the time comes where individual needs and team needs conflict, there is no hesitation: Team First, Me Last.

Word Thought

MISCONCEPTION

*Notes*_____

_____

_____

Old-Timers Football Coaches Week   July 15

The Practice

"If anything goes bad, I did it. If anything goes semi-good, we did it. If anything goes real good, then you did it."

– Coach Paul "Bear" Bryant

The Game

This is a variation of I U WE: I did it. You did it. We did it. Accountability for one's errors and the ability to still feel joy when teammates perform well are the qualities I want in my players. People who are not looking to place blame but are looking to give credit are the kind that separate teams of equal ability.

Word Thought

I U WE

*Notes*_____

_____

_____

Old-Timers Football Coaches Week   July 16

The Practice

"I don't care if my players like me today. I want them to like me when it's important that they like me – when they are out in the world raising families, using their degrees. I want them to like me when it hits them what I've been trying to say all these years."

– Coach Joe Paterno

The Game

You must be able to push and demand and love at the same time. They may not like you all the time, but they will respect you. Do what needs to be done so that when it's done you'll be proud you did it.

Word Thought

CARE

*Notes*_____

_____

_____

Old-Timers Football Coaches Week — July 17

The Practice
"Take the hardest day you have ever worked in your life and make that your average."
– Coach Ed Sherman

The Game
You must build the habit of working hard and then build on that the next day and the next and the next. This was a great thought for me and every day it made me want to get better. I work hard – You work hard – We all work hard: I – U – WE

Word Thought
AVERAGE

*Notes*_____

_____

_____

Old-Timers Football Coaches Week — July 18

The Practice
"3 yards and a cloud of dust"
– Coach Woody Hayes (see Woody Hayes Week, April 14-20)

The Game
This is old-style football that in most people's minds would not work today. However, as a coach you must have a philosophy, a style, a belief, and teach it. Woody adjusted to his changing times and would have adjusted to the demands of today's changing times.

Word Thought
ADJUST

*Notes*_____

_____

_____

July 19

The Practice
Faith is a player who knows his shot will go in when the ball is in the air and the buzzer has gone off.

The Game
You must believe it will go in. Some players live for that moment – some avoid it at all costs. Which are you?

Word Thought
FAITH

*Notes*_____

_____

_____

July 20

The Practice
If we practice with concentration, work hard, have faith in the coach and each other, we can live in peace with our accomplishments.

The Game
Being able to be thoughtful about all circumstances in practice and life will give you the edge you need to succeed.

Word Thought
THOUGHTFUL

*Notes*_____

_____

_____

July 21

The Practice

The player who does not believe in himself cannot believe in anyone else or anything else, for that matter. The coach must believe in himself and the player.

The Game

You must be your own best cheerleader. You can start to believe in yourself if you have paid the price to do so every day in practice.

Word Thought

BELIEVE

*Notes*_____

_____

_____

July 22

The Practice

Coach, do an inventory of everything that is not good for the team and change it or get rid of it.

The Game

You cannot win if you are not in condition to coach, if you do not establish training rules, if you are not learning the game, if you don't lead the team. Are you good for the team?

Word Thought

INVENTORY

*Notes*_____

_____

_____

July 23

The Practice

One of the best things a coach can do for his players is to try to care about and understand their parents.

The Game

"Parents will always love their kids more than they will love the coach." You must understand when they seem unreasonable and trust that what you are doing is good for their child.

– *The Golden Whistle,* Golden Nugget No. 3 "The Dawn Alleviates"

Word Thought

PARENTS

*Notes*_____

_____

_____

July 24

The Practice

The wind toward improvement is always blowing, but you must hoist your own sail.

The Game

You must put yourself in a position to get better by understanding your situation and paying the price. Then you will get better in a breeze.

Word Thought

IMPROVEMENT

*Notes*_____

_____

_____

July 25

The Practice

A positive attitude is the most important practice gear you can wear.

The Game

When you get dressed for practice, put on a smile, a positive lifting attitude. You will change your game and have a positive influence on the rest of the team.

Word Thought

POSITIVE

*Notes*_____

_____

_____

July 26

The Practice

Sweat is the rent you pay for practice.

The Game

You must be willing to lay it on the line, and lay it on the line particularly during the tough conditioning times. Where the sweat flies. the body responds.

Word Thought

SWEAT

*Notes*_____

_____

_____

July 27

The Practice

If you make the same mistake twice, you should be punished. Yes or no?

The Game

We all know we should not repeat mistakes, but that happens. For example, the worst turnover is when you are not aware of what you did to cause the mistake, so it may occur again and again. Awareness is the first step toward correction. Often it takes multiple times to learn enough to stop making the mistake!

Word Thought

MISTAKES

*Notes*_____

_____

_____

July 28

The Practice

As a coach, if you look for the best in your players you will often find the best in yourself.

The Game

You must believe that everyone can get better, that everyone can improve, that everyone you coach is a winner. You can then find great qualities in yourself.

Word Thought

BEST

*Notes*_____

_____

_____

July 29

The Practice

Don't forget that in coaching, a player's greatest emotional need is to feel appreciated.

The Game

Players can tolerate almost anything if they know you really care and appreciate the time, energy and effort they are giving you.

Word Thought
TOLERATE

*Notes*_____

_____

_____

July 30

The Practice

Remember: a winner does what a loser doesn't want to do.

The Game

Long hard practices, extra shooting, leading every sprint, helping teammates, being supportive, are all traits that winners have.

Word Thought
WINNERS

*Notes*_____

_____

_____

July 31

The Practice

When you arrive for practice, let the first thing you say and do brighten the day of everyone around you.

The Game

This is the opposite of "don't rain on someone's parade." Come to practice to be a lifter. The best lifting is done with a smile and a positive attitude. Plus, it's contagious.

Word Thought

CONTAGIOUS

*Notes*_____

_____

_____

Re-read the introduction to the Summer Season.

AUGUST

Find the Gold in the Grind in August: Motivation is an every-day grind. A little motivation today, a little motivation tomorrow and then all of a sudden you reach your big goals and your big dreams. And if you're just waiting for the one big motivation – Yay! Boy! Look at this! Today's The Day! – it's not going to work. This is your chance to communicate and develop relationships with your players (family, friends) year-round. I'm a believer that you take these quotes and make them come alive for your situation; make them relevant to what you're doing. I know it's August, but find a way to keep yourself and the players involved and motivated.

Remember: to get full value, take notes each day. Use the note-taking section after each nugget or have your "Nugget Notebook" at your side.

August 1

The Practice
"They who give have all things; they who withhold have nothing."
– Hindu proverb

The Game
Give until it hurts. Give all you've got. Give 110%. This all sounds good, but is not easy to do. You must not be afraid to give what you have. Don't hold back or wait until tomorrow. This might even sound overwhelming, but you must not be afraid.

Word Thought
GIVE

*Notes*_____

_____

_____

August 2

The Practice

You want joy and happiness? It won't come from winning or losing or great statistics. It will rise up from the contentment of knowing who you are, what you are doing and in what direction you are going.

The Game

You can chase after happiness, but it might be behind you. Instead, set your goals, work hard and find the joy in the journey.

Word Thought

JOURNEY

Notes _____

_____

_____

August 3

The Practice

Practice like you are planting a tree every day. In the same way that, over time, a tree will give you shade, the practice will produce wins.

The Game

Every day you are building toward the future. What you plant today, you reap tomorrow.

Word Thought

PLANT

Notes _____

_____

_____

August 4

The Practice

The great imperative of practice: Practice as if it were your last one.

The Game

You cannot waste any time. The more you can get out of each practice, the more you can put into each game.

Word Thought

IMPERATIVE

*Notes*_____

_____

_____

August 5

The Practice

"Kindness is the language which the deaf can hear and the blind can see."
– Attributed to Samuel Langhorne "Mark" Twain

The Game

We look, but we don't see. We listen, but we don't hear. But when your coaching statements are cloaked in caring, kindness and love, then you are using the universal language that we all understand. The poor player doesn't **hear** how hard he should play on defense and doesn't **see** when a teammate is open.

Word Thought

UNIVERSAL

*Notes*_____

_____

_____

August 6

The Practice

The paradox of practice: if I give until it hurts, there is no more hurt; only progress.
– Mother Teresa (paraphrase)

The Game

Being able to push yourself to new dimensions is a gift that keeps giving day after day. If you truly want to get better, you must push yourself – nobody can do that for you – believing that eventually the pain will give way to progress.

Word Thought

DIMENSIONS

*Notes*_____

_____

_____

August 7

The Practice

Just because you don't get to start or play a lot – Hold on. Hold fast – patience and hard work win the day.

The Game

You may not get all you want today, but by showing tolerance and patience, you will get all you deserve someday.

Word Thought

TOLERANCE

*Notes*_____

_____

_____

August 8

The Practice

You can tell a great practice not so much by where we are today but in what direction we are moving.

The Game

You must be constantly improving. Things may not be looking great today, but if you are determined to make progress, with small steps each day you can achieve your goals.

Word Thought

CONSTANT

*Notes*_____

_____

_____

August 9

The Practice

We know that hard practices produce endurance and that endurance can help you create hope that you can win the game.

The Game

Working hard can help you sustain yourself during long practices, long tough games and long seasons. When you have endurance and hope you are more likely to win.

Word Thought

ENDURANCE

*Notes*_____

_____

_____

August 10

The Practice

A great practice today makes every yesterday's dream possible today and tomorrow's dreams a vision of hope.

– Kālidāsa (paraphrase)

The Game

Dreams are great if they are founded in the reality of daily preparation and learning from mistakes. Only then can tomorrow's hopes be attained.

Word Thought

PREPARE

*Notes*_____

_____

_____

August 11

The Practice

Play the same every day. Let nothing change who you are, neither praise nor discouragement.

– Mother Teresa (paraphrase)

The Game

Do not let other people affect your attitude. Stay the course. Be careful of too much flattery and too many sympathetic voices. Don't crumble to the discouragement of criticism!

Word Thought

FLATTERY

*Notes*_____

_____

_____

August 12

The Practice
Intramurals are full of irreplaceable players.

The Game
You must believe in yourself and have confidence, but you cannot get cocky or too wrapped up in yourself. Work hard to help the team.

Word Thought
COCKY

*Notes*_____

_____

_____

August 13

The Practice
Players often forget what you say in practice and often will forget what drills you did, but they will never forget how you made them feel. Make them feel good about themselves, and you will be successful.

The Game
Whether you win or lose, how you make people feel afterwards will be how they remember you most.

Word Thought
AFTERWARDS

*Notes*_____

_____

_____

August 14

The Practice
Players will often say that a coach was tough and hard on them, that often they didn't even like him at the time. But in reflecting back later on, they often realize how much they learned from the "old" coach about the game and about life.

The Game
Be sure to stand for something. Don't back down from what you believe. Be firm, be fair, be friendly. If you are doing the right things, the players will eventually understand.

Word Thought
REFLECTING

*Notes*_____

_____

_____

August 15

The Practice
If a player is constantly criticized, he will learn to condemn his coach and teammates.

The Game
Be careful with the words that you "shoot" at the players. Fill them with a balance of toughness and love.

Word Thought
WORDS

*Notes*_____

_____

_____

August 16

The Practice

What you say to the players may be the most important part of motivation.

The Game

The use of good verbal cues, like "Good job" and "Well done" and "Good, but we can do better" are amazing catalysts for players to work so they can improve.

Word Thought
CATALYSTS

*Notes*_____

_____

_____

August 17

The Practice

Negative comments can be detrimental to the hopes of players. Tilt the teeter-totter towards positive comments.

The Game

Be careful of saying things like "That was terrible" or "You are awful" or "How stupid can you be." These leave deep scars on players' impressionable minds, and the result can spread from the court to academics and elsewhere in their lives.

Word Thought
DETRIMENTAL

*Notes*_____

_____

_____

August 18

The Practice
It's not just what you say in coaching but the way in which you say it.

The Game
Your body language as a player or a coach can say so much. Be aware of posture and gesturing and facial expressions. These can be just as negative as words.

Word Thought
LANGUAGE

*Notes*_____

_____

_____

August 19

The Practice
A good coach should have a constant, positive, prodding demeanor.

The Game
To develop the trust of the players, constantly show in both words and actions that you trust and believe in them. They will buy into what you are trying to teach.

Word Thought
DEMEANOR

*Notes*_____

_____

_____

August 20

The Practice

If you have taught the values of shared sacrifice and team cohesiveness, then you can keep players believing in you through long and difficult practices or painful losses.

The Game

Teach the values of giving and staying together in the good times and the tough times. Remember – giving gets.

Word Thought

COHESIVENESS

*Notes*_____

_____

_____

August 21

The Practice

Tough, authoritarian-type coaching can bring short-term results but develop long-term resistance.

The Game

This is a controversial statement. You must do what you believe and defend it as a teacher, a leader and a coach who cares and loves.

Word Thought

CONTROVERSY

*Notes*_____

_____

_____

August 22

The Practice

You must nurture a feeling of ownership in the players; make them aware they are responsible for their own improvement.

The Game

The coach can make the players feel good about themselves by showing them ways they can enhance self-improvement. Words of encouragement can do wondrous things. The coach must also be a role model for self-improvement.

Word Thought

ENHANCE

*Notes*_____

_____

_____

August 23

The Practice

"Confidence is the single most important ingredient for athletic success."
– Leif Smith

The Game

Even if you don't agree that it's the single most important ingredient, confidence is certainly something that most athletes can improve on. The coach has an enormous influence in doing that.

Word Thought

CONFIDENCE

*Notes*_____

_____

_____

August 24

The Practice

Most players spend more time worrying about what basketball shoes to buy than they do planning how they can get better.

The Game

Through words and actions, the coach can help players adjust their priorities so they are focusing on the things that will truly help them compete at a higher level.

Word Thought

PRIORITIES

*Notes*_____

_____

_____

August 25

The Practice

Take control of your time. Set up your basketball plans so that you will consistently be working toward higher success.

The Game

Begin small and work your way across the bridge to success. Plan your work, then work your plan. Start today. Do an assessment, find strengths and weaknesses, seek help, and get after it every day.

Word Thought

ASSESS

*Notes*_____

_____

_____

August 26

The Practice
If you want to be more confident, measure your improvements.

The Game
Measure your jumping ability. Measure your bench press progress. Measure your speed. Keep track of your foul shooting and work each day to improve. P.S. Coaches need to measure their improvements beyond wins and losses and beyond player improvements in basketball only.

Word Thought
MEASURE

*Notes*_____

_____

_____

August 27

The Practice
You cannot do the things for players they could and should do for themselves, like academics, getting up for classes or doing homework.

The Game
You must allow the players a degree of freedom to make the kind of choices that they will have to make to be successful after sports.

Word Thought
FREEDOM

*Notes*_____

_____

_____

August 28

The Practice

It is good to have past experiences blended with young hopes.

The Game

Hold on to the past, but keep one hand free to grip on the future. Be open to new ideas, but cling to old principles.

Word Thought

BLENDING

*Notes*_____

_____

_____

August 29

The Practice

Hard practices, easy games. Easy practices, hard games.

The Game

This philosophy shows up time and time again. Practice hard, play better. So much so that it should be easy to believe it.

Word Thought

EASY

*Notes*_____

_____

_____

August 30

The Practice
If your goals are not clear, your results will be havoc.

The Game
You must be clear on where you want to go so that your first steps are in the right direction. You must know where you are going so when you arrive there you know this is where you want to be.

Word Thought
DIRECTION

*Notes*_____

_____

_____

August 31

The Practice
The secret to a good practice is that there are no secrets, only hard work and preparation.

The Game
You must prepare, so that you can utilize time and space. You must motivate, so that the players get the maximum out of each practice.

Word Thought
SECRET

*Notes*_____

_____

_____

Re-read the introduction to the Summer Season.

Summer Season Summary

Review your notes from the Summer Season and reflect on the events and insights that have taken place. Write down your answers to the following three questions on the lines below or in your "Nugget Notebook."

What did you learn from the Summer Season Daily Nuggets?

_____

_____

_____

Are you ready for the Pre-Season?

_____

_____

_____

Which Word Thought was most important for you and why? Keep using that word going forward.

_____

_____

_____

PRE-SEASON

September – October

The summer flew by. School is starting up again. The season is just around the corner. How can you build on the momentum from the summer?

That morning strength and conditioning work leads into individual skill development workouts. The summer pick-up games and the books you read have you fired up about the school year. Are you ready?

Challenge your players to maintain grades and prepare for the next level. Challenge them to find ways to make this consistent and enjoyable.

Understand the concerns and fears that players have at this point: Can I make the team? Might I get cut? Can I play on the varsity? Will I be a starter? How can I help the team? Do I want to play if I'm on the bench?

One of the very rewarding and significant parts of coaching is the opportunity to influence the life journeys of young men and women in all facets of their lives. The relationships, the challenges, the coming together as a team are pivotal at the start of a new school year, whether you're a Division I national contender or a junior high team.

Sharing and discussing *The Daily Nugget* will help everyone come together in a positive, sharing and caring mindset.

What a great time to be a coach! Don't you love the pre-season? The way you start the new school year will go a long way toward becoming a resilient team.

What a challenge, to keep everything in perspective. How's that family doing? Are you including them in your plans?

Ready or not, the season is coming!

SEPTEMBER

Find the Gold in the Grind in September: *Challenge the players to select their own word for the day, either based on the nugget or even one of their own. Have them lead discussions about The Practice and The Game. Encourage them to become a partner with you on the path of becoming the very best that they can be.*

Remember: to get full value, take notes each day. Use the note-taking section after each nugget or have your "Nugget Notebook" at your side.

JOHN WOODEN WEEK
September 1 – 7

Who can argue that he was not the greatest coach of all time? He was a coach and a scholar. I was lucky to have sat beside John and his wife for several years at the NCAA finals.

We had a week on class and character earlier this year. That personified Coach Wooden. Read his book – no, better yet, engage his book, *They Call Me Coach*. It will make you a better coach and a better person.

Have a great week seeking wisdom from the master.

John Wooden Week   September 1

The Practice
"Goals achieved with little effort are seldom worthwhile or lasting."
– Coach John Wooden

The Game
The ability to work hard day after day will provide valuable rewards in the game of basketball, but more importantly, in the game outside of hoops.

Word Thought
ACHIEVEMENT

Notes _____
_____
_____

John Wooden Week   September 2

The Practice

"Although there is no progress without change, not all change is progress."
– Coach John Wooden

The Game

You must adapt to change, but you must be sure that the changes are good and that they fit your circumstances, principles and philosophy.

Word Thought
PROGRESS

*Notes*_____

_____

_____

John Wooden Week   September 3

The Practice

"Do not permit what you cannot do to interfere with what you can do."
– Coach John Wooden

The Game

Coaches must not tell players they can't. Always try and put players in a position where they can succeed. Find something they **can** do. Teach them that when they come up against an obstacle, instead of quitting, they must find a way to go around, over or under the obstacle.

Word Thought
INTERFERE

*Notes*_____

_____

_____

John Wooden Week   September 4

The Practice
"Be more concerned with your character than with your reputation. Character is what you really are; reputation is what others think you are."
– Coach John Wooden

The Game
Be genuine, be sincere, be who you really are and most things will take care of themselves.

Word Thought
REPUTATION

*Notes*_____
_____
_____

John Wooden Week   September 5

The Practice
"Be more concerned with what you can do for others than what you can do for yourself."
– Coach John Wooden

The Game
It is natural to feed our own ego, to be a little selfish. The good teacher-coach is aware of this, allows a degree of freedom, and tries to improve the situation by making players aware of the circumstances.

Word Thought
SELFISH

*Notes*_____
_____
_____

John Wooden Week — September 6

The Practice
"I will get ready, and then, perhaps, my chance will come."
– Coach John Wooden

The Game
The coach and players must have a little faith, a little belief that if they pay the price, it will be worth it. Be ready. Today might be the day. Even when you work hard and prepare, there's no guarantee that you will be a champion. But if you don't work hard and prepare, you are guaranteed to never be a champion.

Word Thought
READY

*Notes*_____

_____

_____

John Wooden Week — September 7

The Practice
"The more concerned we become over the things we can't control, the less we will do with the things we can control."
– Coach John Wooden

The Game
There are times and situations you can't control, like your size, your parents, officials, other players and opponents. But you must step up and take the shot that counts.

Word Thought
CONTROL

*Notes*_____

_____

_____

September 8

The Practice

You may never design a perfect practice, but if you try, you will probably get a lot of excellent ones.

The Game

Never give up on trying to improve your teaching in practice. The better you prepare, the better chance you have to excel.

Word Thought

PERFECTION

*Notes*_____

_____

_____

September 9

The Practice

One of the true tests of courage is not to have lost but to try and win right after you have lost.

The Game

Losing with class takes courage. Preparation to win again after the loss adds class and shows the true essence of what courage really is.

Word Thought

COURAGE

*Notes*_____

_____

_____

September 10

The Practice

If you write your goals down on paper, it's easier for your dreams to come true.

The Game

Your dreams will be like fairy tales until you write them down and take proper steps to achieve them. Be a dreamer at night, a doer in daytime.

Word Thought

WRITE

*Notes*_____

_____

_____

September 11

The Practice

Practicing without a plan or vision is ludicrous. Having a plan without practicing hard is foolish.

The Game

Plan your work, then work your plan. It may seem silly, but you must do both to see your dreams achieved.

Word Thought

LUDICROUS

*Notes*_____

_____

_____

September 12

The Practice

Persistence is when you practice poorly one day and can't wait for practice tomorrow.

The Game

You can't get discouraged with poor performance. Concerned, yes; more determined, yes; fired up, yes. Come to the next practice more excited and good things will happen.

Word Thought

PERSISTENCE

*Notes*_____

_____

_____

September 13

The Practice

When a player practices hard once, not much change occurs. When he practices hard day after day, month after month, year after year, a metamorphosis occurs.

The Game

Constant daily challenges will result in small daily changes that you do not see until the weeks and months, even years, have passed.

Word Thought

METAMORPHOSIS

*Notes*_____

_____

_____

September 14

The Practice

If you do not find time in the off-season to prepare for winning, you will have to prepare to find time for losing.

The Game

With so many things fighting for your time in the off-season, it is difficult indeed to adequately prepare in the way that you should and want to. The warning is clear, however. Prepare to win or prepare to lose.

Word Thought

WARNING

*Notes*_____

_____

_____

September 15

The Practice

My stance shows I'd rather die than give up an open shot or let them by for a lay-up.

The Game

Proper conditioning and a mentally tough attitude will improve your mindset. You can set the defensive tone for the entire squad.

Word Thought

TOUGHNESS

*Notes*_____

_____

_____

September 16

The Practice
Some players can run faster, jump higher and shoot better than everyone else, but no player has the corner on ambition, desire and hustle.

The Game
When you are mentally tougher and more disciplined than your opponents, you can put yourself in a great position. Your attitude can be a great equalizer.

Word Thought
EQUALIZER

*Notes*_____

_____

_____

September 17

The Practice
The practice itself does nothing, neither good nor bad. How you execute the practice, how hard you work, how well you concentrate – now **that** can bring about all kinds of changes.

The Game
You can have the best-ever designed practice, but it won't be any good unless the players are motivated to execute it. How will you motivate them?

Word Thought
EXECUTE

*Notes*_____

_____

_____

September 18

The Practice

Defense the weak player, defense the strong player, defense every possession like it's the last one.

The Game

You must play defense with a great passion and great determination. Give up nothing easily. Make them earn everything.

Word Thought

DEFENSE

*Notes*_____

_____

_____

September 19

The Practice

Your self-discipline is the thermostat that controls all your reactions and regulates all success and failure.

The Game

When you have worked hard to develop and properly regulate your self-discipline, then no matter what the temperature of the game, you will have the same presence of mind and demeanor.

Are you hot tonight and can't miss a shot? You won't get over-excited. Are you cold tonight and can't make a shot? Your disappointment won't influence the rest of your performance. Whether you're hot, cold, or just average, your attitude will remain positive and committed.

This carries over in all areas of the game, your studies and in life. You must control the way you react in all situations.

Word Thought

THERMOSTAT

*Notes*_____

_____

_____

September 20

The Practice

You must get better every day in some small way. Either mentally or physically find some improvement. You win small victories and build your bridges toward success.

The Game

You must find a way to take incremental steps every day, even little baby steps, to get you across the bridge. A lot of small steps can have huge results.

Word Thought

INCREMENTAL

Notes_____

_____

_____

September 21

The Practice

A poor player is not the one who can't jump or shoot or pass very well, but rather the one who believes he can't get better.

The Game

You must be able to keep your dream alive. Not so much where your team is now, but where your team is going. A good coach knows how to step in and help the players believe in themselves and keep their dream alive.

Word Thought

BELIEVE

Notes_____

_____

_____

September 22

The Practice

Dreams are the foundation that will allow us to build our bridges toward improvement in the game and in life.

The Game

We must first believe in ourselves and have a very clear vision of where we want to go, and then dream our dreams.

Word Thought
FOUNDATION

*Notes*_____

_____

_____

September 23

The Practice

Coaches, parents and teachers must be role models for the players and also show confidence in them; then they, in turn, will start to have confidence in themselves.

The Game

Patience, kindness and love are all great attitudes to show players. This behavior helps them feel good about themselves and raises their confidence levels.

Word Thought
MODEL

*Notes*_____

_____

_____

September 24

The Practice

"A teacher [coach] affects eternity; he can never tell where his influence stops."
– Henry Adams

The Game

The younger the player, the more chance you have to really influence him or her. It is an awesome responsibility to be a positive influence.

Word Thought

INFLUENCE

*Notes*_____

_____

_____

September 25

The Practice

You cannot be a role model unless you know where you are going and who you want to lead.

The Game

You must embody the kind of philosophy and principles you wish to instill in your players.

Word Thought

INSTILL

*Notes*_____

_____

_____

September 26

The Practice

Setting long-term and short-term goals will lead you to the bridge you need to cross, but only hard work will get you across.

The Game

Having goals is imperative for success. You must know where you are going. But in order to get there, you need to put on your practice gear, lace up your tennies, and get after it.

Word Thought
IMPERATIVE

*Notes*_____

_____

_____

September 27

The Practice

You must be able to connect the difficult practices to the difficult games.

The Game

Think a little about that statement: It's hard to lift, to run, to sweat if you are not sure why you are doing so. The good coach makes the players aware of what is coming.

Word Thought
PERSPECTIVE

*Notes*_____

_____

_____

September 28

The Practice
The greatest reward for hard work in life and in practice is not what you receive but what the team might become.

The Game
Hard work will always be rewarded, particularly if it is with altruistic thought in mind. Working for the great goals and for the team is a rewarding experience.

Word Thought
ALTRUISM

*Notes*_____

_____

_____

September 29

The Practice
Developing skills in practice should be directly related to how well the players manage these skills in the game.

The Game
You need to develop in players an awareness of what they must do in the game. Having the confidence and freedom to make critical decisions on their own is paramount. These abilities are implanted during practice.

Word Thought
PARAMOUNT

*Notes*_____

_____

_____

September 30

The Practice

Like the habit of shooting the ball correctly, a positive mental attitude must be worked on every day.

The Game

Nothing will happen in one day, or in one week, but sustained concentration and effort can improve your attitude, just like it improves your shot.

Word Thought

SUSTAINED

Notes_____

_____

_____

Re-read the introduction to the Pre-Season.

OCTOBER

Find the Gold in the Grind in October: If you just have a gold nugget in your hand, it's not worth anything until you exchange it for something you value. What do you value in life? I value making players better, I value making coaches and teams better, I value making myself better, I value enriching my life and making my family better. I've taken a nugget and made it truly gold in my life. You can change your nuggets into gold. The gold is the way your heart feels, the way your players feel, the way people feel about you and the way you feel about them.

Remember: to get full value, take notes each day. Use the note-taking section after each nugget or have your "Nugget Notebook" at your side.

October 1

The Practice

You must work on your skills every day. That builds proper habits, which leads to confidence.

The Game

You must have the patience to do things correctly every day, which develops good habits, including the ability to do difficult things easily. All of this will build your confidence. It begins with patience, patience and repetition.

Word Thought

REPETITION

*Notes*_____

_____

_____

October 2

The Practice

As a coach and as a player, you must ask yourself daily, "What am I going to do today to make the team and myself better?"

The Game

Whether you are a coach or a player, before every practice you must gather yourself mentally and physically and know what you want to accomplish that day.

Word Thought
PURPOSE

*Notes*_____

_____

_____

October 3

The Practice

This coaching thing is over-rated unless you are teaching the players to know more about themselves, helping them grow as players and people, and teaching them to work together to make the team the best that it can be.

The Game

Often we are totally consumed by winning. I have been guilty of this. But you must look for the concomitant learnings to find satisfaction in being a positive long-lasting influence.

Word Thought
CONCOMITANT[2]

*Notes*_____

_____

_____

---

[2] "Concomitant" means "associated learnings." Example #1: If you work hard, the associated learning is self-discipline. Example #2: Basketball is about fundamentals, but the associated learning of trust, caring and teamwork, is invaluable.

October 4

The Practice
If you are not happy on the second team, you may not be happy as a starter.

The Game
You must be able to find some contentment and maintain your excitement in every situation you find yourself. Never stop wanting to be the best, but be a lifter in all positions, no matter where you are. You may need the second teamers' support someday yourself.

Word Thought
CONTENTMENT

*Notes*_____

_____

_____

October 5

The Practice
Design your practices, run your patterns, teach your fundamentals, but keep in mind – you cannot play the game for them; they must do that for themselves.

The Game
You must have some control, but you must let the players have the freedom to express themselves – players cannot be afraid to make mistakes. Are you a long-leash coach or a short-leash coach? Dog-gone, it really matters.

Word Thought
FREEDOM

*Notes*_____

_____

_____

October 6

The Practice

Don't be afraid to make mistakes. It's hard to grow if you confine yourself.

The Game

Trying to please the coach or parents is good, but it puts a lot of pressure on you. Do your best, believe yourself, and you will be rewarded. To truly grow, you must believe in yourself and the coach.

Word Thought

PRESSURE

*Notes*_____

_____

_____

October 7

The Practice

The ball often bounces off the rim and you miss the big shot, but your true measure will be how high you bounce back after a miss or a tough loss.

The Game

You will lose sometimes, and you must be ready to bounce back. The tough times won't stay if you decide they won't.

Word Thought

BOUNCE

*Notes*_____

_____

_____

October 8

The Practice
Watching basketball or talking about how good you are is easy. It's tough going to practice, getting in your stance, working your butt off, but it's worth it.

The Game
Why is the game so difficult at times when it should be fun? Look at life – it can be tough. How you handle the tough times will determine how good the 'good times' will be.

Word Thought
DIFFICULT

*Notes*_____

_____

_____

October 9

The Practice
The best players lift the other players. It's not about developing big muscles but about developing big hearts.

The Game
The strength of the team is not always measured by how much you bench press, but by how much you help the team when you come off the bench.

Word Thought
STRENGTH

*Notes*_____

_____

_____

October 10

The Practice
The harder you work on defense, the harder it becomes to score on you.

The Game
You receive back what you give out. Hard work and toughness will help on those key possessions when one stop may win the day.

Word Thought
POSSESSIONS

*Notes*_____

_____

_____

October 11

The Practice
If you are a second teamer, be the best second teamer you can be. Study the first teamers, learn from them and the coach. Then, when your chance comes, you will be the best first teamer you can be.

The Game
There is nothing wrong with not being a starter. Some of the very best players have worked their way up by being the best they could be where they were.

Word Thought
STARTER

*Notes*_____

_____

_____

October 12

The Practice

Coaches can dominate players, but they can't dominate long if they don't have knowledge of the game.

The Game

Even the term 'dominate' sounds negative. To build confidence, you must know what you are doing and share the knowledge with the players.

Word Thought

DOMINATE

*Notes*_____

_____

_____

October 13

The Practice

It's not enough to know how to shoot; one must know how to make a shot and how to miss one.

The Game

Technique is good and proper mechanics are important; however, the courage to take the critical shot is truly a gift.

Word Thought

COURAGE

*Notes*_____

_____

_____

PARADOX WEEK
October 14 – 20

What is a paradox? You may have to look it up to get the definition. This is one of my strongest habits: I look up any word I don't understand. Then I engage it by using it that day. When I was teaching and coaching, I'd use it in the classroom and during practice. Now I use it in my writing and working with coaches.

No time to look up a word? Look it up anyway!

This is a great week to look at yourself and decide to do whatever is necessary to become the best you can be!

Paradox Week   **October 14**

The Practice
Parents and coaches can all be crazy, out of control, ego-laden. Love each other anyway.
– Kent M. Keith, "The Paradoxical Commandments" (paraphrase)

The Game
Conflicts are inevitable – you must continue to give, to listen, to love and not to wave your beating stick at each other.
– Beating stick reference: *The Golden Whistle,* Golden Nugget No. 5 "Put the Beating Stick Down"

Word Thought
CONFLICTS

*Notes*_____

_____

_____

Paradox Week — October 15

The Practice

If you have a great game or a great season, people will accuse you of selfish ulterior motives. Be great anyway.

– Kent M. Keith, "The Paradoxical Commandments" (paraphrase)

The Game

You may be accused of being a ball hog or being concerned only about yourself. If your heart is right, continue to do the best you can. Your accusers will come around if your heart is right.

Word Thought

ACCUSE

*Notes*_____

_____

_____

Paradox Week — October 16

The Practice

When you are on top, you will win false friends and true enemies. Be successful anyway.

– Kent M. Keith, "The Paradoxical Commandments" (paraphrase)

The Game

People will jump on the bandwagon when you win and jump off when you lose. If you have lots of wins, people will be jealous. Be aware that this will happen and continue to succeed.

Word Thought

BANDWAGON

*Notes*_____

_____

_____

Paradox Week   October 17

The Practice

The coach of the year award, the all-league and all-American awards will be forgotten tomorrow. Do your best anyway.

– Kent M. Keith, "The Paradoxical Commandments" (paraphrase)

The Game

Snap your fingers; it goes so fast. But if you have done the best you can in a manner that has class, then it is worth everything.

Word Thought

CLASS

*Notes*_____

_____

_____

Paradox Week   October 18

The Practice

What you spend years building as a coach and player may be lost in an instant. Build your dreams anyway.

– Kent M. Keith, "The Paradoxical Commandments" (paraphrase)

The Game

You must have character, but be aware that a lot of people will want to drag you down. Stand tall when the challenges present themselves. It can all be lost with one bad choice.

Word Thought

CHALLENGES

*Notes*_____

_____

_____

Paradox Week   October 19

The Practice
Players really need and want your help, but may challenge your motives if you lose. Help them anyway.
– Kent M. Keith, "The Paradoxical Commandments" (paraphrase)

The Game
You will be attacked by people. Expect this. Try and understand this, never hold a grudge, and continue to do the best you can. What are your motives?

Word Thought
MOTIVES

*Notes*_____

_____

_____

Paradox Week   October 20

The Practice
Even if you coach the best you can you may get your butt kicked. Give the game the best you have anyway.
– Kent M. Keith, "The Paradoxical Commandments" (paraphrase)

The Game
Nobody can win them all or be a hero in every practice or every game. But when you're down, look around a little. Help those who are down there with you and then get your butt back up.

Word Thought
KICKED

*Notes*_____

_____

_____

October 21

The Practice

You must be able to control yourself or you cannot control others.

The Game

Poor or abusive language shows lack of control. Dick Hopkins, a high school coach, posted a sign in his locker room which read, "PROFANITY SHOWS A LACK OF VOCABULARY." Discipline your thoughts and actions so that when the players emulate you, they have a positive role model.

Word Thought

ABUSIVE

*Notes*_____

_____

_____

October 22

The Practice

What you do is not as important as the conviction with which you act. Do not waver in your coaching technique or philosophy.

The Game

You must be decisive. There will be a lot of pressure on you. Make your decisions and stand behind them. This does not mean to be rigid and stop listening. On the contrary, you must always be ready to adapt to changing circumstances, but don't crumble over outside pressure.

Word Thought

CONVICTION

*Notes*_____

_____

_____

October 23

The Practice
You cannot put too much in the minds of players or it will slow their feet.

The Game
Keep it simple. How many times have we heard this? As a coach, it's not what you know but what you can get the players to understand and then execute.

Word Thought
CONFUSION

*Notes*_____

_____

_____

October 24

The Practice
The truly good coach cares deeply about how the players do in practice and the games, but more importantly, wants them to succeed in life.

The Game
Caring about more than just how your players play is really an important part of coaching. Getting to know them, their families, their likes and dislikes, will develop a lifelong bond, which is essential to team development.

Word Thought
ESSENTIAL

*Notes*_____

_____

_____

October 25

The Practice

Leadership is a great privilege and responsibility. What can give your life more meaning than helping others?

The Game

Whether you are a coach or a player, nothing should give you more satisfaction than helping others. If no one cares who gets the credit, everybody can improve.

Word Thought

PRIVILEGE

*Notes*_____

_____

_____

October 26

The Practice

As a coach, you must be able to see what a player could be. You must not look at what is, but what might be.

The Game

Being able to see potential and possibilities and then work with the players to realize their potential is rewarding indeed.

Word Thought

POTENTIAL

*Notes*_____

_____

_____

October 27

The Practice
Caring is important to the team. It lifts not only the ones that receive, but also the one who gives.

The Game
It is important to care about each other. Giving up yourself for the benefit of the team is a lofty goal and yields deep satisfaction.

Word Thought
CARING

*Notes*_____

_____

_____

October 28

The Practice
One of the secrets of good coaching is to forgive the players of all mistakes every day and start fresh the next day.

The Game
It is easy to harbor bad thoughts after a hard practice or a tough loss. Look at the stats, check the video, incorporate what you've learned, then forget the past and prepare for the future.

Word Thought
FORGIVE

*Notes*_____

_____

_____

October 29

The Practice
Practice the little things with great concentration.

The Game
It is important for the coach to sell the players on how important it is that the "little" details actually make a "BIG" difference.

Word Thought
DETAILS

*Notes*_____

_____

_____

October 30

The Practice
It is your responsibility to practice hard, not because you have to, but because you want to.

The Game
This axiom is particularly true during the off-season when no one is watching. You must be motivated from within to practice hard every day. This is just as true for coaches, who must plan, study and learn during the off-season.

Word Thought
AXIOM

*Notes*_____

_____

_____

October 31

The Practice

If you are not sure you want to practice, a tough practice could destroy you. If you have a strong will and resolve about practice, no matter how tough the practice is, it will only make you better.

The Game

If you want to get better, if you want to help the team, if you look forward to practice then you are on the path for improvement.

Word Thought

RESOLVE

*Notes*_____

_____

_____

Re-read the introduction to the Pre-Season.

Pre-Season Summary

Review your notes from the Pre-Season and reflect on the events and insights that have taken place. Write down your answers to the following three questions on the lines below or in your "Nugget Notebook."

What did you learn from the Pre-Season Daily Nuggets?

_____

_____

_____

Are you ready for the Early Season?

_____

_____

_____

Which Word Thought was most important for you and why? Keep using that word going forward.

_____

_____

_____

EARLY SEASON

November – December

It's here! The first practice jitters are behind us. Our first scrimmage is this week. We open in two weeks. It's the same game as pre-season, but the pressure is pumped up. Hearts beat faster, first teams are assigned, subs are designated and each group needs solid coaching.

Clearly communicate your aspirations and goals to the players and to their parents. Some parents have already indicated displeasure with their son or daughter's playing time. Are you ready for this?

Were you good last year? Are you picked to win your league or conference? Can you handle the added pressure?

This is for real. The record will go in the books and your job may be on the line. Win or lose, maintain the perspective of a coach who cares about the players. *The Daily Nugget* will keep you and your players directed.

Coaching is a great profession because it challenges you and the players to get better every day.

- Thanks for being a coach.
- Thanks for being a player.
- Thanks for being a parent.
- Thanks for being an official.
- Thanks for helping me in my mission to improve the game of basketball.
- Thanks for making basketball a great game.

November to March – it's pucker time!

"Remember, it's better to be on top, being shot at,
than at the bottom doing the shooting."

Ed Sherman

NOVEMBER

Find the Gold in the Grind in November: The practices must reflect the games. Practice every day like you are preparing to play the best team on your schedule to win it all. The practices will seem like a grind, but you are really polishing your skills for the season.

Remember: to get full value, take notes each day. Use the note-taking section after each nugget or have your "Nugget Notebook" at your side.

November 1

The Practice
You don't want practices that are not tough, or that don't challenge you. Without effort there is no change. Without change you fall behind.

The Game
You want a coach who will be demanding, who will push you, who makes you work on fundamentals, and conditions you to get better. The tougher the conditions, the tougher you become.

Word Thought
TOUGHNESS

Notes_____
_____
_____

November 2

The Practice

Talking about getting better is easily ignored. Working hard every day in practice cannot be resisted.

The Game

It is easy to talk about doing the right thing. Don't let your mouth write checks your body won't cash. Walk the walk and talk the talk.

Word Thought

IGNORED

*Notes*_____

_____

_____

November 3

The Practice

The giving of yourself in practice for the team should never be a sacrifice – it should be a privilege. If you look at it as sacrifice, the giving will never be total or complete.

The Game

If you are worried about giving up free time or time spent with friends, then it will be difficult to give everything you have to practice and the team.

Word Thought

PRIVILEGE

*Notes*_____

_____

_____

November 4

The Practice

It is the giving of everything one has with enthusiasm and joy that makes the difference between the exceptional and the excellent.

The Game

Pure joy and enthusiasm can be contagious. It will spread throughout the entire team. This kind of giving becomes the highest expression of the word 'team.'

Word Thought

EXCEPTIONAL

*Notes*_____

_____

_____

November 5

The Practice

If we want to cross the bridge and get to new places in our game, it can only be through the the absolute giving of ourselves to the other players on the journey.

The Game

Helping each other, caring for each other, lifting each other, leading each other, will help direct us to new levels of team play.

Word Thought

CROSSING

*Notes*_____

_____

_____

November 6

The Practice

The team may play great, but to be great we must care about each other and be motivated by kindness and love.

The Game

The team, the team – my winning for the team. We need to improve the individuals so they can help the team. Carry an ounce of kindness with you at all times.

– William Shakespeare (paraphrase)

Word Thought

KINDNESS

*Notes*_____

_____

_____

November 7

The Practice

A player's worth should not be judged by whether he is starting but whether he is getting better each day.

The Game

Players must keep trying to get better, to work hard, to help the team, rather than worry too much about playing time.

Word Thought

WORTH

*Notes*_____

_____

_____

November 8

The Practice
How you finish a practice, a game or a season is more important than how you start it.

The Game
You can't get discouraged too soon. Hang in there and often good things will happen. Be proud that you stayed the course.

Word Thought
DISCOURAGED

*Notes*_____

_____

_____

November 9

The Practice
Be careful not to measure the kind of season you are having until it is over.

The Game
A lot of seasons can be turned around if you stay focused and continue to improve. You cannot let negative thoughts overwhelm you. On the other hand, seasons can turn down in an instant if you let a strong start make you lazy or inattentive.

Word Thought
OVERWHELM

*Notes*_____

_____

_____

November 10

The Practice

You may not be the most talented, but if you can develop persistence, you will always be in the game.

The Game

Those who refuse to give in or give up even when things are going badly are difficult to beat. You knock them down and look around and they are standing up again.

Word Thought

PERSISTENCE

*Notes*_____

_____

_____

November 11

The Practice

You can't go back and make yesterday's bad practice or bad day better, but you sure can make today's practice or day a great one.

The Game

Don't worry too much about yesterday. Evaluate it, think about it, and then make plans to make today the best you can.

Word Thought

YESTERDAY

*Notes*_____

_____

_____

WHY TEAMS UNDERACHIEVE WEEK
November 12 – 18

This week talks about why teams underachieve. Coaches, you should replace the word 'team' with the word 'coach' each day. Coaches also underachieve and this can cause teams to underachieve. Be sure that you are not an underachieving coach.

You must want to improve every year, not just in the X's and O's, but in all areas of relationship skills. You may not believe this, but when you work on relationship skills, your X's and O's will also improve! Build your program on solid steps that will lead to over-achieving for the team and for the coach!

Why Teams Underachieve Week   **November 12**

The Practice
Teams underachieve because they have low intrinsic motivation and get frustrated if the coach pushes them.

The Game
The coach and players must be on the same wavelength. Both must be self-motivated and yet connected so they have a single purpose.

Word Thought
INTRINSIC

*Notes*_____

_____

_____

Why Teams Underachieve Week   November 13

The Practice

Teams underachieve because players involved have other priorities and don't apply themselves during practices.

The Game

If you are thinking about other parts of your life during practice, it's not possible for you to reach the level of concentration you need to get better.

Word Thought

CONCENTRATION

*Notes*_____

_____

_____

Why Teams Underachieve Week   November 14

The Practice

Teams underachieve because they hold back effort which often is due to fear of failure.

The Game

A lot of players don't want to give everything just in case they don't make it. Then they have a built in excuse. Don't be afraid to fail; be afraid of not giving it your all.

Word Thought

AFRAID

*Notes*_____

_____

_____

The Practice
Teams underachieve because the players will not work on their own; they only work when someone is watching.

The Game
Each player must be willing to work hard in pre-practice, in post-practice, even when at home. You must accept the responsibility to make the team better.

Word Thought
RESPONSIBILITY

*Notes*_____

_____

_____

The Practice
Teams underachieve because the coach has them try to do too much and they become disorganized.

The Game
Back to 'keep it simple.' Do what the players are capable of doing and not more. Keep the players' minds free to execute the fundamentals.

Word Thought
DISORGANIZED

*Notes*_____

_____

_____

Why Teams Underachieve Week — November 17

The Practice
Teams underachieve because the players can't get along with each other.

The Game
The good teams will sacrifice to make sure the team gets along. No cliques, no personal agendas; all for one and one for all.

Word Thought
SACRIFICE

*Notes*_____

_____

_____

Why Teams Underachieve Week — November 18

The Practice
Teams underachieve because they do not believe they can win.

The Game
The only way to develop confidence is by being clear with your goals, working hard and winning. You may need a little time for the last one, but the first two should be constant, because without them, you'll never win.

Word Thought
CONSTANT

*Notes*_____

_____

_____

November 19

The Practice
The toughest player on your squad is not much tougher than the weakest player but he is tougher on the last sprint, in the last conditioning drill, at the end of practice.

The Game
We all hurt, we all feel like we can't go on. That's when the best rise up and give that great effort that sets the apart and makes them leaders.

Word Thought
EFFORT

*Notes*_____

_____

_____

November 20

The Practice
It's difficult to beat a team whose players never give up, whose heart beats as one and who really care about each other.

The Game
Never, never, never give up. Stay together and fight the good fight. These are lofty goals, indeed, but worth striving for.

Word Thought
LOFTY

*Notes*_____

_____

_____

November 21

The Practice

When you're missing your shots and your opponents are making all of theirs, hang in there. Things change and you must be ready when they do.

The Game

There will be days and games when things just don't go your way. Hang tough. Show resilience and you will be prepared when things turn. And they always do.

Word Thought

RESILIENCE

*Notes*_____

_____

_____

November 22

The Practice

If you are willing and eager for the practice, the difficulties seem to disappear.

The Game

If you love to practice, love the chance to work hard and get better, the practices, like life, will fly by.

Word Thought

DIFFICULTIES

*Notes*_____

_____

_____

November 23

The Practice
We all have about the same amount of time to practice, but it's what you do with that time that makes all the difference.

The Game
You must be organized and motivated to utilize the time you have. If everyone is on the same page, it will all go better.

Word Thought
ORGANIZED

*Notes*_____

_____

_____

November 24

The Practice
"We are what we repeatedly do. Excellence, then, is not an act but a habit."
– Will Durant

The Game
Repetition is boring, but is the only way to develop the habits that will win for you in those pressure moments we all dream about. Can you teach "Do it again?"

Word Thought
BORING

*Notes*_____

_____

_____

November 25

The Practice

The team can accomplish great things if they stick together long enough.

The Game

Long practices, tough drills, scrimmages and games can make for long tough times. Stick together and good things will happen.

Word Thought

STICK

*Notes*_____

_____

_____

November 26

The Practice

When we lose, a lot of people point fingers. The good coach holds out his hand and helps point the players in the right direction.

The Game

Losing will always bring the doubters out. This is when the coach and players cannot blame each other. They need to reach out and lift each other.

Word Thought

DOUBTERS

*Notes*_____

_____

_____

November 27

The Practice

It is easy to find fault with a player's game. Instead, you must be looking for a way to make them better and to encourage them to be all they can become.

The Game

Coach, players and parents can find fault very easily. But to see potential or possibilities and then to work hard to get better – that's what it is all about.

Word Thought

ENCOURAGE

*Notes*_____

_____

_____

November 28

The Practice

Teamwork can be an overused term, but when things are difficult, it is great to know that someone is on your side and that you will all stick together.

The Game

We must be a cohesive unit – players coaches, fans and parents because things often go wrong – injuries, losses, bad calls, mistakes. But if we are part of something bigger, held together by caring, the sun will soon shine again.

Word Thought

COHESIVE

*Notes*_____

_____

_____

November 29

The Practice

The blending of different talents and personalities into the best team can be one of the great joys in life.

The Game

The coach has an awesome responsibility: to bring players together so they can operate for a single purpose, that of becoming the best they are capable of.

Word Thought
RESPONSIBILITY

*Notes*_____

_____

_____

November 30

The Practice

Two players were asked where they were going. One said, "To practice." The other said, "To make myself a better player and help the team."

The Game

It is easy to fall into the trap of just practicing. You must have goals that can help you get better. Be intentional every day. You must have a direction every day. Have a purpose or reason to practice hard.

Word Thought
INTENTIONAL

*Notes*_____

_____

_____

Re-read the introduction to the Early Season.

DECEMBER

Find the Gold in the Grind in December: Finals are coming! Finals are coming! Be sure you and the players keep things in perspective. Practices, games, classes, and family must each have proper attention. Be careful of too much pressure and stress. Be aware and help the players help themselves.

Remember: to get full value, take notes each day. Use the note-taking section after each nugget or have your "Nugget Notebook" at your side.

December 1

The Practice
The coach must try to have the team come together. That is the beginning. He must keep them working together. That is a long process. Then he must get them to work together to achieve ultimate success. That is unending.

The Game
Helping each other from the beginning of practice though the tough season to success is worth the effort. Stay in pursuit of your goals.

Word Thought
SUCCESS

Notes_____

_____

_____

December 2

The Practice

If you want to become a better player or a better coach, start on the inside with your heart and head. The body will follow.

The Game

It is easy to think that you want to be a better shooter, scorer or passer; or that you want to be more patient or understanding as a coach, but that is difficult to achieve if you don't get your heart into it and your head screwed on right. Right heart, right head: this is paramount.

Word Thought
PARAMOUNT

*Notes*_____

_____

_____

December 3

The Practice

Great teams are born only from the union of everyone working with each other and cooperating with each other.

The Game

The more you do things together, the closer you become and the better the chances are of you reaching your full potential as a team.

Word Thought
COOPERATING

*Notes*_____

_____

_____

December 4

The Practice

What are the players on this team willing to do in order to become an even better team?

The Game

Are you willing to play on the second team, not be a starter, not be the leading scorer? What are you willing to give so that the team can fully achieve?

Word Thought

WILLING

*Notes*_____

_____

_____

December 5

The Practice

A good team player will give 100% effort on and off the court, make very few mental errors, care about the team above all else and demonstrate loyalty to coach and teammates.

The Game

We all want to be a team player. However, like most good things, we must be prepared to work for it, to strive for it, to make it our personal goal! The team first!

Word Thought

DEMONSTRATE

*Notes*_____

_____

_____

December 6

The Practice

Team – <u>T</u>ogether <u>E</u>veryone <u>A</u>ccomplishes <u>M</u>ore. Bob Tucker, my head coach at Marysville (Ohio) High School, kept this on the bulletin board.

The Game

Such a simple quote that says so much. We must have a sense of community, of caring, and respect for each other. When no one cares who gets the credit, a great deal can be accomplished.

Word Thought

ACCOMPLISH

*Notes*_____

_____

_____

December 7

The Practice

You are going to lose some. You are going to get your feelings hurt. It is part of the great opportunity to compete.

The Game

Be careful when you don't start, or the coach takes you out, and your feelings get hurt. Beware of sympathy from friends and parents. Disappointments are the part of the game that can make you better or worse.

Word Thought

DISAPPOINTMENT

*Notes*_____

_____

_____

December 8

The Practice

Respect your teammates, because it is through them that you will be motivated through difficult practices and games.

The Game

You must love to go to practice and prepare for the games. If you truly care about the other players on the team, the time spent can really be enjoyable.

Word Thought

TEAMMATES

*Notes*_____

_____

_____

December 9

The Practice

In the great game of basketball, in the locker room and on the court, nothing creates teamwork like great effort from the heart.

The Game

If you give a great effort and support your teammates and coach, the spirit you give will be contagious.

Word Thought

CONTAGIOUS

*Notes*_____

_____

_____

December 10

The Practice

A little less of YOU and ME and a little more of US.

The Game

This is a great thought for success – to make the players into a true team will require the best ingredients: YOU and ME will equal US. Another way to say this is I – U – WE.

Word Thought

I – U – WE

*Notes*_____

_____

_____

December 11

The Practice

Teamwork is like a pass in basketball. It must be given with no thought of receiving it back.

The Game

Passing to someone for a lay-up or open shot is a great thrill. We call that an assist. It is important to give that assist with no thought of getting one back, knowing deep down that it is better to give than to receive.

Word Thought

GIVE

*Notes*_____

_____

_____

December 12

The Practice
Just as the strength of the pack is the wolf and the strength of the wolf is the pack, we will be better if we work together.
– Rudyard Kipling (paraphrase)

The Game
Kipling's quote inspired this thought that I know to be true: The strength of the team is its defense and the strength of the defense is the team.

Word Thought
STRENGTH

*Notes*_____

_____

_____

December 13

The Practice
The challenge is to experience each moment with a clear mind and open heart. When you do that, the game and life will take care of themselves.

The Game
To stay in the moment in practice and in the game will prepare you to stay in the moment in life. Conversely, to stay in the moment in life will prepare you to stay in the moment in practice and the game.

Word Thought
CONVERSELY

*Notes*_____

_____

_____

December 14

The Practice

Everyone has a plan to be a starter, until they aren't.

The Game

When reality sets in and you are not getting to play as much as you want, you must be mentally tough. Don't get down on yourself but be up for all the situations life throws at you.

Word Thought

MENTAL

*Notes*_____

_____

_____

December 15

The Practice

The principle seems simple to follow: play hard and smart when you have the ball; play hard and smart when you don't.

The Game

You must be consistent and not play on just one end of the floor. The really great players never take a play off.

Word Thought

SMART

*Notes*_____

_____

_____

December 16

The Practice

If you are tough, that sets the tone for your teammates to be tough. I get tough, you get tough, we get tough. I – U – WE.

The Game

It is often said that the team reflects the personality of the coach. I believe this is true. They also reflect the personality of each other.

Word Thought

TOUGHNESS

*Notes*_____

_____

_____

WORK WEEK
December 17 – 23

Players must be taught how to work hard. The best way to do that is if they see the coach putting in the hours on and off the court. The coach must push himself first. Only then can he successfully push players so they can grow and blossom into becoming great players. This is the key to becoming a great team.

Work your way through Work Week. It should be fun!

Work Week   **December 17**

The Practice
"Man's finest hour – his greatest fulfillment to all he holds dear – is that moment when he has worked his heart out in a good cause and lies exhausted on the field of battle – victorious."
– Coach Vince Lombardi

The Game
This is a super quote. When one is exhausted following a great game, win or lose, it can be your finest moment, for to give all you have is victory.

Word Thought
EXHAUSTED

*Notes*_____

_____

_____

Work Week — December 18

The Practice
Talent alone is no assurance of success. The only way to assure you will get better is through long hours of hard work.

The Game
Be careful that having talent doesn't make you arrogant or cocky or wrapped up in yourself. This will make it difficult to push yourself to your highest level.

Word Thought
ASSURANCE

*Notes*_____

_____

_____

Work Week — December 19

The Practice
You want to stand out? Work out more than any of your teammates and your opponents.

The Game
There are very few athletes who are willing to put forth an all-out effort day in and day out to get better. All coaches love players who stand out by their efforts.

Word Thought
EFFORTS

*Notes*_____

_____

_____

The Practice

Every day that you fail to practice hard, to work extra, you miss a great opportunity to improve.

The Game

You need to develop your weaknesses into strengths and make your strengths ever stronger. You can do this by working hard each day.

Extra! Extra! Read all about it! Coach improves, player improves, and team improves!

Word Thought
EXTRA

*Notes*_____

_____

_____

The Practice

There will be areas where the opponents may have an advantage over us. Conditioning should never be one of these.

The Game

Conditioning is about work. It's about toughness. It's about an attitude that we will be the best-conditioned team – period.

Word Thought
CONDITIONING

*Notes*_____

_____

_____

December 22

The Practice
The best way to be in the best condition is to never get out of it.

The Game
The pre-season, the off-season, the pre-practice, the post-practice – these are the times that the great players, the great teams, take advantage of.

Word Thought
ADVANTAGE

*Notes*_____

_____

_____

December 23

The Practice
Anything you do that will harm your body will reduce your conditioning and reduce your chances for success.

The Game
Don't do anything that will hurt your chances of playing or the team's chances of success.

Word Thought
SUCCESS

*Notes*_____

_____

_____

December 24

The Practice

If you work hard in practice when the coach wants you to, the day will come when you can do the things you want to do in the game.

The Game

You must pay the price so you can experience what it is like to be able to execute your fundamentals during a game.

Word Thought
EXECUTE

*Notes*_____

_____

_____

COACHING TIP FROM COACH BURSON:

Have a joyful Christmas Eve and Christmas Day. Be sure to follow the Work Week theme for the rest of the season. It should be a labor of love.

December 25

The Practice

The greatest reward for hard work and concentration in practice is not what you get for it, but what you become because of it.

The Game

The habit of self-discipline that you learn from sports is often like a shadow – it will follow you the rest of your life. It is a gift that will keep giving! Merry Christmas!

Word Thought
REWARD

*Notes*_____

_____

_____

December 26

The Practice
Praying for a win is good, but your chances are increased if you have also practiced hard and well.

The Game
Doing just what is expected is good, but doing more, pushing yourself, going the extra mile can make all the difference and separate you and your team from your competitors.

Open the gift of extra effort every day.

Word Thought
PUSHING

*Notes*_____
_____
_____

December 27

The Practice
There is very little traffic on the extra mile.

The Game
Good job, nice practice, see you tomorrow. Do you stay and work extra? Are you never satisfied? Where you are now is good, but you always want to go further and get better.

Word Thought
EXTRA

*Notes*_____
_____
_____

December 28

The Practice

If you want to get ready for next season, the best time to start is today.

The Game

Often a lot of players will say, "I'm going to shoot 500 shots starting tomorrow." The best time to start is today. There is no exchange policy. Once you don't shoot, it is gone forever.

Word Thought

TOMORROW

*Notes*_____

_____

_____

December 29

The Practice

Workouts are not utilized to the fullest by most players because they're dressed in sweats, look like work and don't feel like a game.

The Game

One day of conditioning is as important as the last. The effort of that first holiday practice must be sustained day after day through the entire season. That first holiday practice sets the tone for success.

Word Thought

SUSTAIN

*Notes*_____

_____

_____

December 30

The Practice

Good things often come to those who wait, but good offense and defense most often come to those who hustle.

The Game

It is good to be patient and wait for opportunities, but it is great fun to hustle your butt and go capture the day.

Word Thought

HUSTLE

*Notes*_____

_____

_____

December 31

The Practice

When you study, really study; when you play, play hard.

The Game

My high school coach, Bob Tucker, gave this to me when I left for college. It is still on my bulletin board today. This is great to put on your bulletin board. Don't carry the practice or the game to class with you. Be a great student, study hard, and when practice comes, discipline yourself to concentrate on making yourself a better player. Happy New Year!

Word Thought

CONCENTRATE

*Notes*_____

_____

_____

Re-read the introduction to the Early Season.

Early Season Summary

Review your notes from the Early Season and reflect on the events and insights that have taken place. Write down your answers to the following three questions on the lines below or in your "Nugget Notebook."

What have you learned so far from the Daily Nuggets for the Early Season?

_____

_____

_____

Are you ready for the rest of your season?

_____

_____

_____

Which Word Thought was most important for you and why? Keep using that word going forward.

_____

_____

_____

> **COACHING TIP FROM COACH BURSON:**
>
> *Don't forget your family. Keep things in perspective. Keep a monitor on yourself and your team. My resolve is simply to become the best I can be. The best is yet to come.*

ACKNOWLEDGMENTS

I am grateful to everyone who has helped this book become a reality. I began six years ago and today it is in a form that I couldn't have dreamed of back then.

I want to start by thanking Charlie Gilkey of Productive Flourishing. Two years ago Jennifer and I thought we would offer these nuggets in the form of an emailed subscription product. Charlie, our business coach, said, "Absolutely not. This needs to be a book!" He was right, of course. But my second book, *The Golden Whistle – Going Beyond: The Journey to Coaching Success,* was published first. And I'm proud to say that this first book (fondly referred to for many months as Book #2) is being published exactly twelve months later.

Thank you to those who gave their time, energy and talents to help clarify and improve the book: Joe "Jersey" Arganbright, Pat Campbell, Joanna Duncan, Judy Haselhoef, Valerie Lyle, Janice McCloud, Don McKendry, Alan Pakaln and Glenn Wikes.

Thank you to my family and friends who guided and directed me way before the book and continue to support me: to my children and grandchildren, my sisters and brother and their families, my wife's family, and our many friends.

I'm especially grateful for the support from these four people: Tim Berger seems to be single-handedly bringing *The Golden Whistle* before every high school basketball coach in Ohio. Every time I have a new idea, I bring it to Andy Clark, whose tremendous basketball mind takes my ideas and enriches them. Kathy Smith kept me sane and employed while I was teaching and coaching; she also prepared the very first conception of *The Daily Nugget* from my yellow legal pad scribbles. George Klein has been that friend I could turn to at any time over the past 50 years.

My thanks to the JETLAUNCH Strategic Publishing team. Chris O'Byrne, Debbie O'Byrne and all the other folks at this fantastic company have guided us in both books through the perils and pitfalls of this new world of publishing with kindness, patience and expert direction.

Finally, my heartfelt gratitude and thanks to all the players, parents and fans who have been there through the wins and losses, and to everyone who loves the game, especially the coaches.

THANK YOU FOR READING

Dear Reader,

Thank you for reading and, hopefully, engaging *The Daily Nugget*. Read, study and engage the game of basketball and the game of life. Make yourself better every day.

I will. You will. We will.

Now I'd like you to take your engagement up a notch and ask you to review *The Daily Nugget* on Amazon. Even a short review helps — just a word or two about what you'd tell someone who's thinking of reading it. Directions for posting reviews are at the end of this letter.

If you know someone who might benefit from the ideas in *The Daily Nugget*, please send them a copy as a gift or share your copy.

If you'd like to order the book for your team, organization, company or book club (over 50 copies,) go to www.jimburson.com/contact.

If you're interested in keynotes or workshops based on *The Daily Nugget* or *The Golden Whistle*, go to www.jimburson.com/contact.

Finally, if you'd like to get my free blog and get updates on my future projects, you can sign up at www.jimburson.com.

Thanks very much. Keep digging and turn your nuggets into gold!

Coach Burson

P.S. To post a review, go to Amazon.com. Search for the book by title or author. At the top of the book page, where the title is, you'll see a link called "Customer Reviews." Click on that link. On the next page, just under the gold stars, you'll see "Share your thoughts with other readers" and "Create your own review." Click there and you'll be able to type your comments.

QUOTE AND PARAPHRASE REFERENCES

JANUARY 11

A gem cannot be polished without friction, nor a player perfected without trials.

– Chinese proverb (paraphrase)

Original: "nor a man perfected without trials"

FEBRUARY 13

There can never be true conversation, no true relationship, between a player and a coach, until each talks in terms of the team.

– Ralph Waldo Emerson, "Friendship" (paraphrase) *Essays: First Series* (1841)

Original: "There can never be deep peace between two spirits, never mutual respect, until in their dialogue each stands for the whole world."

FEBRUARY 14

You must love and respect other coaches, but be careful not to study their ideas so much that you lose your own.

– Ralph Waldo Emerson, "Friendship" (paraphrase)

Original: "Then though I prize my friends, I cannot afford to talk with them and study their visions, lest I lose my own."

FEBRUARY 15

Winning has its tax, and if it comes without work and sweat, it has little virtue; the next game will blow it away!

– Ralph Waldo Emerson, "Compensation" (paraphrase) *Essays: First Series* (1841)

Original: "Material good has its tax and if it came away without desert or sweat, has no root in me and the next wind will blow it away."

FEBRUARY 16

Winning reduces blame as surely as the sun melts the iceberg in the sea.

– Ralph Waldo Emerson, "Compensation" (paraphrase)

Original: "Love reduces inequalities as the sun melts the iceberg in the sea."

FEBRUARY 17

The question of how to coach resolves itself into a practical question of my conduct!! How should I live?

– Ralph Waldo Emerson, "Fate" (paraphrase) *Conduct of Life* (1860)

Original: "To me, the question of the times resolved itself into a practical question of the conduct of life. How shall I live?"

FEBRUARY 18

The fate of the team may be determined by a coach who thanks his bench and stands in some terror of his starters.

– Ralph Waldo Emerson, "Fate" (paraphrase)

Original: "A man must thank his defects and live in some terror of his talents."

MARCH 12

"The man of genius is he and he alone who finds such joy in his art that he will work at it come hell or high water."

– Marie-Henri Beyle (1783-1842), best-known by his pen name Stendhal, French writer

MARCH 14

"Do not trust to the cheering, for those very persons would shout as much if you and I were going to be hanged."

– Oliver Cromwell (1599-1658), English military leader and later Lord Protector of the Commonwealth

MARCH 19

I can give you three surefire ways to avoid being criticized: Do nothing. Say nothing. Be nothing.

– Elbert Hubbard (1856-1915), American publisher and writer

Original: "Do nothing, say nothing and be nothing, and you'll never be criticized." Probably from *John North Willys – Pamphlet* published in the late 1890's by his Roycroft Press. **Encyclopædia Britannica Online**, s. v. "Elbert Hubbard", accessed December 06, 2014, http://www.britannica.com/EBchecked/topic/274472/Elbert-Hubbard.

MARCH 20

"Nothing in the world can take the place of persistence. Talent will not; nothing is more common than unsuccessful men with talent .... Persistence and determination alone are omnipotent."

– Calvin Coolidge (1872-1933), 30th President of the United States

Attributed to Coolidge; appeared on the program cover of a 1933 memorial service for him. The Forbes Library, Northampton, Massachusetts has searched its Coolidge collection for this. *Respectfully Quoted: A Dictionary of Quotations Requested from the Congressional Research Service.* Washington D.C.: Library of Congress, 1989; Bartleby.com, 2003. www.bartleby.com/73/.

POST-SEASON: APRIL-MAY

"Spectacular achievement is always preceded by unspectacular preparation."

– Robert Schuller (b. 1924)

Author of *36 books; founding pastor of Crystal Cathedral*

APRIL 2

"Nothing splendid has ever been achieved except by those who dared believe that something inside them was superior to circumstances."

– Bruce Barton (1886-1967), American advertising executive, author and politician, from "The Executive," *The Man Nobody Knows* (1925)

APRIL 8

The happiest coaches are those who have harvested their time in others. The unhappiest coaches are those who wonder how the game is going to make them happy.

– John C. Maxwell (paraphase) (b. 1947), American author and speaker

Original: "The happiest people are those who have harvested their time in others. The unhappiest people are those who wonder how the world is going to make them happy."

APRIL 11

Defense and rebounding are a matter of hustle, desire and pride more than anything else.

– Tex Winter (paraphase) (b. 1922), Hall of Fame basketball coach and creator of the Triangle Offense

Original: "Good defensive play is as much a matter of hustle, desire and pride as it is anything else."

APRIL 13

There are some pigs in this world. Remember this rule: "Don't ever wrestle with a pig. You both get dirty and the pig likes it."
– Attributed to George Bernard Shaw (1856-1965), Nobel Prize and Academy Award-winning Irish writer and author of the play *Pygmalion* (1912) which was made into the musical *My Fair Lady* (1956)

APRIL 14-20: WOODY HAYES WEEK

– Wayne Woodrow "Woody" Hayes (1913-1987), Hall of Fame football coach, Ohio State University 1951-1978

APRIL 21

"Sometimes a player's greatest challenge is coming to grips with his role on the team."
– Scottie Pippen (b. 1965), two-time inductee into the Naismith Basketball Hall of Fame, only person to have won the NBA title and Olympic gold medals in the same year, two times (1992, 1996.)

APRIL 26

When one eye is constantly fixed on winning, there is only one eye left with which to find the best way.
– Zen saying (paraphrase)

Original: "When one eye is fixed upon your destination, there is only one eye left with which to find the Way.

APRIL 30

"Use the past as a springboard, not a sofa."
– Harold Macmillan (1894-1986), Prime Minister of the United Kingdom 1957-1963

MAY 2

"The masters all have the ability to discipline themselves to eliminate everything except what they are trying to accomplish."
– Coach Dale Brown (b. 1935), Hall of Fame basketball coach, author, speaker, Louisiana State University 1972-1997

MAY 3

"What you get by reaching your goals is not nearly as important as what you become by reaching them."
– Hilary Hinton "Zig" Ziglar (1926-2012), author and motivational speaker
See You At the Top, Gretna: Pelican Pub. Co. (1975)

MAY 10

One of the first things you must do is to develop proper work habits. The ability to stick to something when it gets difficult comes from doing it over and over. You develop the habit of not giving up or giving in. *"Do it 4,999 times and then once more!"*
– Dr. Forrest Clare "Phog" Allen (1885-1974), Hall of Fame basketball coach who played for and coached after James Naismith at the University of Kansas

MAY 14-20: MICHAEL JORDAN WEEK

– Michael Jordan (b. 1963), two-time Hall of Fame inductee, named by the Associated Press second to Babe Ruth in list of the top athletes of the 20th century, two-time Olympic Gold Medal, played 15 NBA seasons for the Chicago Bulls and Washington Wizards, principal owner of the Charlotte Hornets, the first-ever billionaire athlete (according to *Forbes*)

http://en.wikipedia.org/wiki/Michael_Jordan

MAY 22

The longer you coach, the more you need to adjust to changing times, and yet you must cling to unchanging principles.
– Julia Coleman (paraphrase) (d. 1973), teacher and superintendent in Plains, Georgia, quoted in the inaugural address of Jimmy Carter (b. 1924), 39th President of the U.S. and Nobel Peace Prize recipient

Original: "We must adjust to changing times and cling to unchanging principles."

MAY 24

"It is not the critic who counts; not the man who points out how the strong man stumbles, or where the doer of deeds could have done better. The credit belongs to the man who is actually in the arena."
– Theodore Roosevelt (1851-1919), 26th President of the United States

Excerpt from the speech "Citizenship in the Republic" delivered at the Sorbonne in Paris on April 23, 1910

JUNE 1

"Very little is needed to make a happy life; it is all within yourself, within your way of thinking."

– Marcus Aurelius (121-180 CE), Emperor of Rome, Stoic philosopher

Meditations, Book VII

JUNE 10

"Fame is a vapor, popularity an accident, riches take wings. Only one thing endures – character."

– Horace Greeley (1811-1872), founder, editor, publisher of the *New York Tribune* newspaper; he is generally credited with the phrase "Go West, young man, go West," and he did use it in an editorial, but the actual originator was an Indiana journalist, John Soule.

Encyclopædia Britannica Online, s. v. "Horace Greeley", accessed December 07, 2014, http://www.britannica.com/EBchecked/topic/244839/Horace-Greeley.

JUNE 17

"People are always blaming their circumstances for what they are. I don't believe in circumstances. People with character are the ones who get up and look for the circumstances they want and, if they can't find them, make them."

– George Bernard Shaw (1856-1965), Nobel Prize and Academy Award-winning Irish playwright; from *Mrs. Warren's Profession* (1893), Act II.

JUNE 18

When you are angry, moderation is a virtue. When you are defending your principles, moderation is a vice.

– Thomas Paine (paraphrase) (1737-1809), English-American essayist whose writings, particularly his pamphlet *Common Sense,* influenced the American Revolution.

Original: "Moderation in temper is always a virtue; but moderation in principle is always a vice." *The Political Writings of Thomas Paine* (1830 edition), accessed December 07, 2014, http://izquotes.com/quote/140920

JULY 12

"Build for your team a feeling of oneness, of dependence on one another and of strength to be derived by unity."

– Coach Vince Lombardi (1913-1970), Hall of Fame coach of the Green Bay Packers 1959-67, never had a losing season. The Super Bowl trophy is named the Vince Lombardi Trophy.

JULY 13

"Don't forget your fundamentals – fundamentals in the game and fundamentals in life."

– Coach Tony Dungy (b. 1955), championship coach of the Tampa Bay Buccaneers (1996-01) and Indianapolis Colts (2001-08), best-selling author, NBC analyst

JULY 14

"There is a misconception about teamwork. Teamwork is the ability to have different thoughts about things; it's the ability to argue and stand up and say loud and strong what you feel. But in the end, it's also the ability to adjust to what is best for the team."

– Coach Tom Landry (1924-2000), Hall of Fame coach Dallas Cowboys (1960-88), 20 consecutive winning seasons, inventor of "4-3" defense

JULY 15

"If anything goes bad, I did it. If anything goes semi-good, we did it. If anything goes real good, then you did it."

– Coach Paul "Bear" Bryant (1913-1983), Hall of Fame coach, University of Alabama (1957-83), National Coach of the Year Award is named after him

JULY 16

"I don't care if my players like me today. I want them to like me when it's important that they like me – when they are out in the world raising families, using their degrees. I want them to like me when it hits them what I've been trying to say all these years."

– Coach Joe Paterno (1926-2012), Hall of Fame coach, Penn State Nittany Lions 1966-2011

Sports Illustrated, "A Good Joe," August 21, 2008 http://www.si.com/vault

JULY 17

"Take the hardest day you have ever worked in your life and make that your average."

– Coach Ed Sherman (1912-2009), first Division III coach inducted into the College Football Hall of Fame, coach of Muskingum University Fighting Muskies 1945-66

JULY 18

"3 yards and a cloud of dust"

– Coach Woody Hayes (see Woody Hayes Week, April 14-20)

This trademark quote refers to his belief in the running game and that a consistent play is one that gains at least three yards. "Origin of Three Yards and a Cloud of Dust" http://ohiostate.247sports.com Accessed December 07, 2014

AUGUST 5

"Kindness is the language which the deaf can hear and the blind can see."

– Attributed to Samuel Langhorne "Mark" Twain (1835-1910), author of *The Adventures of Tom Sawyer, Adventures of Huckleberry Finn* and other iconic works

AUGUST 6

The paradox of practice: if I give until it hurts, there is no more hurt; only progress.

– Mother Teresa (paraphrase) (1910-1997), Nobel Peace Prize recipient, humanitarian and missionary, Roman Catholic religious sister

Original: "I have found the paradox, that if you love until it hurts, there can be no more hurt, only more love."

AUGUST 10

A great practice today makes every yesterday's dream possible today and tomorrow's dreams a vision of hope.

– Kālidāsa (paraphrase) (370-450 AD), Sanskrit writer, poet, dramatist

Original: *Look To This Day*, "For yesterday is but a dream and tomorrow is only a vision; and today well-lived, makes yesterday a dream of happiness and every tomorrow a vision of hope."

AUGUST 11

Play the same every day. Let nothing change who you are, neither praise nor discouragement.

– Mother Teresa (paraphrase)

Original: "If we were humble, nothing would change us – neither praise nor discouragement. If someone were to criticize us, we would not feel discouraged. If someone would praise us, we also would not feel proud."

AUGUST 23

"Confidence is the single most important ingredient for athletic success."
– Leif Smith, author and founder of Personal Best Consulting

"A Blueprint for Building Confidence" accessed on December 07, 2014, www.person-albestconsulting.com/article-6

SEPTEMBER 1-7: JOHN WOODEN WEEK

– Coach John Wooden (1910-2010), Presidential Medal of Freedom, Naismith Hall of Fame as player and as coach, inaugural member of Collegiate Hall of Fame, coach of UCLA 1948-75

SEPTEMBER 24

"A teacher (coach) affects eternity; he can never tell where his influence stops."
– Henry Adams (1838-1918), historian and author, descended from Presidents John and John Quincy Adams

The Education of Henry Adams, Chapter XX "Failure", (published privately 1907; published posthumously by Houghton and won a Pulitzer Prize)

PARADOX WEEK: OCTOBER 14-17

Paraphrases are based on the "The Paradoxical Commandments®," first published by Kent M. Keith in his 1968 booklet for student leaders, *The Silent Revolution: Dynamic Leadership in the Student Council. Anyway: The Paradoxical Commandments: Finding Meaning in a Crazy World* (G.P. Putnam's Sons: 2002). Accessed December 07, 2014, *www.paradoxicalcommandments.com*

OCTOBER 14

Parents and coaches can all be crazy, out of control, ego-laden. Love each other anyway.
– Kent M. Keith, author and speaker, "The Paradoxical Commandments" (paraphrase)

Original: "People are illogical, unreasonable and self-centered. Love them anyway."

OCTOBER 15

If you have a great game or a great season, people will accuse you of selfish ulterior motives. Be great anyway.
– Kent M. Keith, "The Paradoxical Commandments" (paraphrase)

Original: "If you do good, people will accuse you of selfish ulterior motives. Do good anyway."

OCTOBER 16

When you are on top, you will win false friends and true enemies. Be successful anyway.

– Kent M. Keith, "The Paradoxical Commandments" (paraphrase)

Original: "If you are successful, you will win false friends and true enemies. Succeed anyway."

OCTOBER 17

The coach of the year award, the all-league and all-American awards will be forgotten tomorrow. Do your best anyway.

– Kent M. Keith, "The Paradoxical Commandments" (paraphrase)

Original: "The good you do today will be forgotten tomorrow. Do good anyway.

OCTOBER 18

What you spend years building as a coach and player may be lost in an instant. Build your dreams anyway.

– paraphrase of Kent M. Keith

Original: "What you spend years building may be destroyed overnight. Build anyway."

OCTOBER 19

Players really need and want your help, but may challenge your motives if you lose. Help them anyway.

– Kent M. Keith, "The Paradoxical Commandments" (paraphrase)

Original: "People really need help but may attack you if you do help them. Help people anyway."

OCTOBER 20

Even if you coach the best you can you may get your butt kicked. Give the game the best you have anyway.

– Kent M. Keith, "The Paradoxical Commandments" (paraphrase)

Original: "Give the world the best you have and you'll get kicked in the teeth. Give the world the best you have anyway."

EARLY SEASON: NOVEMBER-DECEMBER

Coach Ed Sherman (1912-2009), first Division III coach inducted into the College Football Hall of Fame, coach of Muskingum University Fighting Muskies 1945-66

NOVEMBER 6

The team, the team – my winning for the team. We need to improve the individuals so they can help the team. Carry an ounce of kindness with you at all times.

– paraphrase of William Shakespeare (1564-1616) "The Bard of Avon," playwright and poet

Original: *Richard III, Act 5, Scene 4;* "A horse! A horse! My kingdom for a horse!"

NOVEMBER 24

"We are what we repeatedly do. Excellence, then, is not an act but a habit."

– Will Durant (1885-1981), historian and philosopher, Presidential Medal of Freedom, Pulitzer Prize with his wife, Ariel, for *The Story of Civilization*

The Story of Philosophy: The Lives and Opinions of the World's Great Philosophers (1926) Simon & Schuster, Chapter II "Aristotle and Greek Science", usually misattributed to Aristotle, the Greek philosopher and scientist.

DECEMBER 12

Just as the strength of the pack is the wolf and the strength of the wolf is the pack, we will be better if we work together.

– Rudyard Kipling (paraphrase)

Original: "For the strength of the pack is the wolf and the strength of the wolf is the pack." *The Law of the Wolves,* Rudyard Kipling (1865-1936), Nobel Prize-winning English poet and novelist, well-known in the U.S. for *The Jungle Book.*